Emotional Abuse

Gaslighting, Narcissistic Abuse, Co-Dependency, Toxic Relationships

Cathleen R. Barton

I0092683

Emotional Abuse: Gaslighting, Narcissistic Abuse, Co-Dependency, Toxic Relationships

Table of Contents

Book 1 - Gaslighting

A Survivor's Guide to Healing and Empowerment After Psychological Abuse

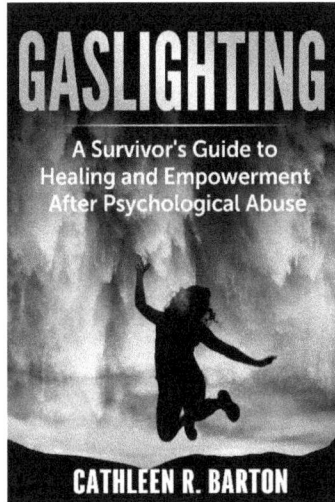

01: What is Gaslighting?

Gaslighting is a form of psychological manipulation in which a person or group seeks to sow seeds of doubt in a targeted individual or group, making them question their own memory, perception, or judgment. It is a tactic often used by abusers, dictators, and cult leaders to control and subjugate their victims. The term "gaslighting" comes from the 1938 stage play "Gas Light," in which a husband tries to drive his wife crazy by dimming the gas lights in their home and then denying that the light changed when his wife points it out.

There are several tactics that are commonly used in gaslighting. One is denial, in which the manipulator flatly denies that something happened or that they said something, even when there is clear evidence to the contrary. This can leave the victim feeling confused and uncertain, and they may begin to question their own recollection of events.

Another tactic is lying and exaggerating, in which the manipulator makes false or exaggerated claims about the victim or about events that have occurred. This can cause the victim to doubt their own perception of reality and to feel that they are unreliable or untrustworthy.

Manipulators may also use the tactic of withholding information, in which they selectively provide or withhold information in order to confuse and mislead the victim. This can
make it difficult for the victim to understand what is happening and can leave them feeling isolated and unsure of
whom to trust.

A manipulator may also use the tactic of manipulating physical evidence, such as altering documents or hiding objects,
in order to support their claims and create confusion. This
can leave the victim feeling uncertain and unsure of what is
true.

One of the most insidious tactics of gaslighting is projection,
in which the manipulator accuses the victim of the very
things that they themselves are guilty of. For example, an
abuser may accuse their victim of being manipulative or abusive, even though it is the abuser who is behaving that way.
This can leave the victim feeling confused and unsure of
their own actions, and can be especially effective in causing
the victim to doubt their own judgment.

The effects of gaslighting can be devastating, as it can leave the victim feeling confused, isolated, and unsure of their own perceptions and judgment. It can also cause the victim to become more dependent on the manipulator, as they may come to rely on them for a sense of stability and guidance. In extreme cases, gaslighting can lead to the victim developing mental health problems such as anxiety, depression, and PTSD.

It is important to recognize the signs of gaslighting and to seek help if you or someone you know is being victimized in this way. Some common signs include feeling confused or unsure of what is happening, feeling isolated or cut off from support, and feeling like you are going crazy. If you suspect that you or someone you know is being gaslighted, it is important to seek help from a trusted friend, family member, or mental health professional. It is also important to remember that you are not alone and that there is support available.

It is important to remember that gaslighting is a form of abuse, and it is never the fault of the victim. The manipulator is solely responsible for their actions, and it is important to hold them accountable for their behavior.

01: WHAT IS GASLIGHTING?

If you are being gaslighted, it is important to try to maintain a sense of reality and to seek out supportive relationships with friends and family members who can help you to stay grounded and to feel confident in your own perceptions and judgment. It can be helpful to keep a journal or a record of events, as this can help you to better understand what is happening and can serve as evidence if you need to seek help or report the abuse.

It is also important to remember that you have the right to set boundaries and to assert your own needs and wants. This may be difficult if you are being gaslighted, as the manipulator may try to control your behavior and limit your autonomy. However, it is important to stand up for yourself and to assert your own rights and needs. This may involve seeking help from a therapist or counselor, or it may involve seeking support from friends and family members.

If you are in an abusive relationship and are being gaslighted, it may be necessary to leave the relationship in order to protect yourself and your well-being. This can be a difficult and frightening decision, but it is important to remember that you deserve to be treated with respect and to be in a healthy, safe relationship. There are resources available to help you leave an abusive relationship, such as domestic violence shelters and hotlines, and it is important to reach out for help if you need it.

In conclusion, gaslighting is a harmful and abusive tactic that is used to manipulate and control others. It can have serious effects on the victim's mental health and well-being, and it is important to recognize the signs of gaslighting and to seek help if you or someone you know is being victimized in this way. Remember that you are not alone, and that there is support available to help you heal and to regain control over your life.

It is also important to remember that gaslighting is not just something that happens in personal relationships. It can also occur in professional settings, such as the workplace or in political contexts.

In the workplace, a manager or colleague may use gaslighting tactics to undermine an employee's confidence and to make them question their own abilities or judgment. This can be especially harmful if the employee is isolated or lacks support from their colleagues.

In political contexts, gaslighting can be used as a tactic to manipulate public opinion and to spread misinformation. This can be especially dangerous, as it can erode trust in institutions and undermine the foundations of democracy.

It is important to be aware of the potential for gaslighting in all types of relationships and to be alert to the signs of manipulation. It is also important to support and empower those who may be victims of gaslighting, and to hold manipulators accountable for their actions.

It is worth noting that it is possible for someone to gaslight themselves, particularly if they have low self-esteem or a history of being manipulated or abused. In these cases, it can be helpful to seek therapy or counseling to work through these issues and to build a stronger sense of self-worth and self-confidence.

Overall, gaslighting is a harmful and insidious form of manipulation that can have serious consequences for the victim. It is important to be aware of the signs of gaslighting and to seek help if you or someone you know is being victimized in this way. Remember that you deserve to be treated with respect and to be in healthy, supportive relationships, and that there is help available to support you in achieving this.

02: The Signs of Gaslighting

Gaslighting is a form of psychological manipulation that can be difficult to recognize, especially if you are in a close relationship with the manipulator. However, there are several signs that can indicate that you or someone you know is being gaslighted.

One of the most common signs of gaslighting is feeling confused or unsure of what is happening. The manipulator may deny or distort events, or may withhold information, in order to create confusion and uncertainty. As a result, the victim may feel like they are "going crazy" or like they can't trust their own perceptions.

Another sign of gaslighting is feeling isolated or cut off from support. The manipulator may try to isolate the victim from friends and family, or may try to undermine their relationships with others, in order to make them more reliant on the manipulator. This can leave the victim feeling alone and unsure of whom to trust.

A third sign of gaslighting is feeling like you are constantly second-guessing yourself or doubting your own judgment. The manipulator may try to undermine the victim's confidence in their own abilities or judgment, and may try to make them feel incompetent or incapable. This can leave the victim feeling insecure and unsure of themselves.

A fourth sign of gaslighting is experiencing a change in your personality or behavior. The manipulator may try to control the victim's behavior or to make them conform to their expectations, and this can lead to the victim changing their personality or behavior in order to please the manipulator.

A fifth sign of gaslighting is experiencing a change in your relationships with others. The manipulator may try to alienate the victim from their friends and family, or may try to manipulate the victim's relationships with others in order to further their own goals. This can leave the victim feeling isolated and alone.

It is worth noting that not all of these signs necessarily indicate that someone is being gaslighted. However, if you are experiencing several of these signs, or if you are feeling confused, uncertain, or isolated, it may be worth considering the possibility that you are being manipulated.

It is important to remember that if you are being gaslighted, it is not your fault. The manipulator is solely responsible for their behavior, and it is important to hold them accountable for their actions. If you are in an abusive relationship and are being gaslighted, it may be necessary to leave the relationship in order to protect yourself and your well-being.

There are resources available to help you leave an abusive relationship, such as domestic violence shelters and hotlines, and it is important to reach out for help if you need it.

If you suspect that you or someone you know is being gaslighted, it is important to seek help from a trusted friend, family member, or mental health professional. It is also important to remember that you are not alone and that there is support available to help you heal and to regain control over your life.

It can be especially difficult to recognize the signs of gaslighting if you are in a close relationship with the manipulator, as they may have gained your trust and may have convinced you that they have your best interests at heart. However, it is important to be aware of the potential for manipulation and to be alert to the signs that something may be wrong.

Some other signs of gaslighting to watch out for include:

– The manipulator consistently contradicts your perceptions or memories of events, even when you are sure you are right.

– The manipulator frequently changes the subject or distracts you when you try to discuss something that is important to you.

– The manipulator minimizes your feelings or concerns, or makes you feel like you are being oversensitive or unreasonable.

– The manipulator tries to make you feel guilty or ashamed for things that are not your fault.

– The manipulator tries to control your behavior or decisions, or makes you feel like you have to ask permission for things.

– The manipulator tries to turn others against you, or undermines your relationships with friends and family.

If you are experiencing these signs, it is important to take them seriously and to seek help if you need it. Remember that you have the right to be treated with respect and to be in healthy, supportive relationships, and that you deserve to feel safe and valued.

It is also important to be aware of the potential for gaslighting in professional or political contexts. In these settings, manipulators may use similar tactics to undermine your confidence, to spread misinformation, or to control public opinion. It is important to be aware of these tactics and to be vigilant against them.

Overall, the signs of gaslighting can be subtle and may not be immediately obvious. However, if you are experiencing confusion, uncertainty, or a sense that something is not right, it is important to trust your instincts and to seek help if you need it. Remember that you are not alone and that there is support available to help you heal and to regain control over your life.

It is also important to recognize that gaslighting is a form of abuse, and it is never the victim's fault. The manipulator is solely responsible for their actions, and it is important to hold them accountable for their behavior.

If you are in a relationship with someone who is gaslighting you, it can be difficult to know what to do. It is important to remember that you have the right to set boundaries and to assert your own needs and wants. This may involve setting limits on the time you spend with the manipulator or on the types of conversations you have with them. It may also involve seeking support from friends and family or from a therapist or counselor.

If you are in an abusive relationship and are being gaslighted, it may be necessary to leave the relationship in order to protect yourself and your well-being. This can be a difficult and frightening decision, but it is important to remember that you deserve to be treated with respect and to be in a healthy, safe relationship. There are resources available to help you leave an abusive relationship, such as domestic violence shelters and hotlines, and it is important to reach out for help if you need it.

It is also important to remember that it is possible to recover from gaslighting and to rebuild your sense of self-worth and self-confidence. This may involve seeking therapy or counseling, or it may involve building new, supportive relationships with friends and family. It is important to be patient with yourself and to give yourself time to heal.

In conclusion, gaslighting is a harmful and abusive tactic that can have serious consequences for the victim. It is important to recognize the signs of gaslighting and to seek help if you or someone you know is being victimized in this way. Remember that you are not alone, and that there is support available to help you heal and to regain control over your life.

03: The Impact of Gaslighting on Your Mental Health

Gaslighting is a form of psychological manipulation in which a person or group seeks to sow seeds of doubt in a targeted individual, making them question their own memory, perception, or judgment. Gaslighting can occur in personal relationships, at work, or in political or social groups. It is often a subtle form of abuse, as the manipulator may try to convince their victim that they are simply misunderstanding things or are overly sensitive. However, the effects of gaslighting can be severe and long-lasting, causing serious damage to a person's mental health and well-being.

One of the most insidious aspects of gaslighting is that it can be difficult to detect, especially if the manipulator is skilled at concealing their true intentions. They may deny saying or doing certain things, or present conflicting information in a way that leaves the victim feeling confused and uncertain. This can lead to the victim feeling isolated and disconnected from their own reality, as they struggle to make sense of what is happening around them.

The constant questioning of one's own perceptions and

memories can be emotionally and mentally exhausting, leading to feelings of anxiety, depression, and low self-esteem. The victim may also feel a sense of powerlessness and helplessness, as they are unable to control the manipulation or stop it from happening. In some cases, they may begin to doubt their own sanity, leading to serious mental health issues such as paranoia, dissociation, and even psychosis.

Gaslighting can also have a profound impact on a person's relationships and social interactions. The manipulator may try to alienate the victim from their friends and family, further isolating them and making it more difficult for them to seek support. The victim may also become more reliant on the manipulator for emotional support, leading to an unhealthy dynamic in which they are constantly seeking validation and approval from their abuser.

There are several ways in which a person can protect themselves from the effects of gaslighting. It is important to be aware of the signs of gaslighting and to trust one's own perceptions and instincts. It can also be helpful to seek support from trusted friends, family members, or a mental health professional. It is also important to set boundaries and to communicate openly and honestly with the manipulator, letting them know that their behavior is not acceptable.

In some cases, it may be necessary to seek help from a legal or social services agency in order to protect oneself from on-going abuse. It is also important to remember that no one deserves to be subjected to gaslighting or any other form of psychological abuse, and that it is never too late to seek help and make positive changes in one's life.

In conclusion, gaslighting is a serious form of psychological manipulation that can have a devastating impact on a person's mental health and well-being. It is important to be aware of the signs of gaslighting and to seek support in order to protect oneself from its harmful effects. With the right help and support, it is possible to break free from the cycle of abuse and to reclaim one's own sense of self and reality.

It is important to recognize that gaslighting is a form of abuse and that it can have serious consequences for a person's mental health. If you suspect that you or someone you know is being gaslighted, it is important to seek help and support.

03: THE IMPACT OF GASLIGHTING ON YOUR MENTAL HEALTH

There are several resources available for individuals who are experiencing gaslighting or other forms of abuse. These may include therapy or counseling, support groups, or legal or social services agencies. These resources can provide the necessary support and guidance to help individuals cope with the effects of gaslighting and to develop healthy coping strategies.

It is also important to remember that it is never too late to seek help and to make positive changes in one's life. No one deserves to be subjected to gaslighting or any other form of abuse, and it is possible to break free from the cycle of abuse and to reclaim one's own sense of self and reality.

It is important to recognize that gaslighting can have serious and long-lasting effects on a person's mental health and well-being. If you or someone you know is experiencing gaslighting or other forms of abuse, it is important to seek help and support as soon as possible. With the right resources and support, it is possible to break free from the cycle of abuse and to rebuild one's sense of self and reality.

It is important to recognize that gaslighting can be a subtle and insidious form of abuse, and that it can be difficult for a

victim to identify and acknowledge what is happening to
them. This can make it difficult for them to seek help and
support, as they may not realize the full extent of the manipulation and abuse they are experiencing.

One of the most important things a victim of gaslighting can
do is to seek support from trusted friends, family members,
or a mental health professional. These individuals can
provide a sense of grounding and help the victim to validate
their own perceptions and experiences. It can also be helpful to seek out a support group or therapy, where the victim
can connect with others who have experienced similar abuse and can learn healthy coping strategies.

It is also important for victims of gaslighting to set boundaries and to communicate openly and honestly with the manipulator. This can help to establish clear expectations and
to assert control over the situation. In some cases, it may be
necessary to seek help from a legal or social services agency
in order to protect oneself from ongoing abuse.

It is also important to remember that it is never too late to
seek help and to make positive changes in one's life. No one
deserves to be subjected to gaslighting or any other form of

abuse, and it is possible to break free from the cycle of abuse and to reclaim one's own sense of self and reality.

In conclusion, the impact of gaslighting on mental health can be severe and long-lasting. It is important to recognize the signs of gaslighting and to seek help and support in order to protect oneself from its harmful effects. With the right resources and support, it is possible to break free from the cycle of abuse and to rebuild one's sense of self and reality.

04: The Cycle of Gaslighting and How to Break Free

The cycle of gaslighting is a pattern of manipulation and abuse that can be difficult for a victim to recognize and break free from. Gaslighting is a form of psychological manipulation in which a person or group seeks to sow seeds of doubt in a targeted individual, making them question their own memory, perception, or judgment. Gaslighting can occur in personal relationships, at work, or in political or social groups. It is often a subtle form of abuse, as the manipulator may try to convince their victim that they are simply misunderstanding things or are overly sensitive.

The cycle of gaslighting typically begins with the manipulator planting seeds of doubt in the victim's mind. This may involve denying saying or doing certain things, or presenting conflicting information in a way that leaves the victim feeling confused and uncertain. The manipulator may also try to alienate the victim from their friends and family, making it more difficult for them to seek support or validation from others.

As the cycle continues, the victim may begin to doubt their own perceptions and memories, leading to feelings of anxi-

ety, depression, and low self-esteem. They may also feel a
sense of powerlessness and helplessness, as they are unable
to control the manipulation or stop it from happening. In
some cases, they may even begin to doubt their own sanity,
leading to serious mental health issues such as paranoia,
dissociation, and psychosis.

The cycle of gaslighting can be difficult to break, as the manipulator may be skilled at concealing their true intentions
and at making the victim feel like they are the problem.
However, there are steps that a victim of gaslighting can
take to break free from this cycle and to reclaim their sense
of self and reality.

One of the most important things a victim of gaslighting can
do is to seek support from trusted friends, family members,
or a mental health professional. These individuals can
provide a sense of grounding and help the victim to validate
their own perceptions and experiences. It can also be helpful to seek out a support group or therapy, where the victim
can connect with others who have experienced similar abuse and can learn healthy coping strategies.

It is also important for victims of gaslighting to set boundaries and to communicate openly and honestly with the manipulator. This can help to establish clear expectations and to assert control over the situation. In some cases, it may be necessary to seek help from a legal or social services agency in order to protect oneself from ongoing abuse.

It is also important for victims of gaslighting to practice self-care and to engage in activities that promote their own well-being. This may include exercising, engaging in hobbies, or seeking out activities that bring them joy and fulfillment. Taking care of oneself can help to build resilience and to provide a sense of stability and purpose, which can be especially important during times of uncertainty and stress.

Breaking free from the cycle of gaslighting can be a challenging and difficult process, but it is possible with the right support and resources. It is important to remember that no one deserves to be subjected to gaslighting or any other form of abuse, and that it is never too late to seek help and make positive changes in one's life. By seeking support and learning healthy coping strategies, victims of gaslighting can break free from the cycle of abuse and reclaim their sense of self and reality.

04: THE CYCLE OF GASLIGHTING AND HOW TO BREAK FREE

It is also important for victims of gaslighting to be aware of the signs of gaslighting and to trust their own perceptions and instincts. This can help them to recognize when they are being manipulated and to seek help and support before the cycle of abuse becomes more entrenched. Some common signs of gaslighting may include:

– Denial of events or actions: The manipulator may deny saying or doing certain things, even when confronted with evidence to the contrary.

– Presenting conflicting information: The manipulator may present conflicting information in a way that leaves the victim feeling confused and uncertain.

– Isolating the victim: The manipulator may try to alienate the victim from their friends and family, making it more difficult for them to seek support or validation from others.

– Diminishing the victim's accomplishments: The manipulator may attempt to belittle or diminish the victim's accomplishments in order to make them feel incompetent or unworthy.

– Blaming the victim: The manipulator may attempt to shift blame onto the victim, making them feel responsible for the manipulator's behavior.

It is important for victims of gaslighting to be aware of these signs and to trust their own perceptions and instincts. If you suspect that you or someone you know is being gaslighted, it is important to seek help and support as soon as possible. With the right resources and support, it is possible to break free from the cycle of abuse and to reclaim your sense of self and reality.

In conclusion, the cycle of gaslighting is a pattern of manipulation and abuse that can have serious and long-lasting effects on a person's mental health and well-being. It is important to be aware of the signs of gaslighting and to seek help and support in order to break free from this cycle. With the right resources and support, it is possible to break free from the cycle of abuse and to reclaim your sense of self and reality. So, it is very important to recognize the signs of gaslighting and take necessary actions to break free from it.

It is also important for individuals who have experienced gaslighting to be mindful of their own mental health and to seek help if needed. The effects of gaslighting can be severe and long-lasting, and it is important to address any mental health issues that may arise as a result of the abuse. This may include seeking therapy or counseling, joining a support group, or seeking help from a mental health professional.

It is also important for individuals who have experienced gaslighting to practice self-care and to engage in activities that promote their own well-being. This may include exercising, engaging in hobbies, or seeking out activities that bring them joy and fulfillment. Taking care of oneself can help to build resilience and to provide a sense of stability and purpose, which can be especially important during times of uncertainty and stress.

It is also important for individuals who have experienced gaslighting to be mindful of their relationships and to surround themselves with supportive and caring individuals. This may involve seeking out new friendships or building healthier relationships with existing friends and family members. It may also be necessary to set boundaries with individuals who are not supportive or who engage in manipulative or abusive behaviors.

Breaking free from the cycle of gaslighting can be a difficult and challenging process, but it is possible with the right support and resources. It is important to remember that no one deserves to be subjected to gaslighting or any other form of abuse, and that it is never too late to seek help and make positive changes in one's life. By seeking support and learning healthy coping strategies, individuals who have experienced gaslighting can break free from the cycle of abuse and reclaim their sense of self and reality.

05: The Role of Boundaries in Healing from Gaslighting

Boundaries are an important aspect of healthy relationships and can play a crucial role in the healing process for individuals who have experienced gaslighting or other forms of abuse. Gaslighting is a form of psychological manipulation in which a person or group seeks to sow seeds of doubt in a targeted individual, making them question their own memory, perception, or judgment. Gaslighting can occur in personal relationships, at work, or in political or social groups. It is often a subtle form of abuse, as the manipulator may try to convince their victim that they are simply misunderstanding things or are overly sensitive.

One of the most harmful effects of gaslighting is that it can leave victims feeling isolated and disconnected from their own reality. They may feel confused and uncertain about what is happening around them, and may struggle to trust their own perceptions and instincts. Setting boundaries is an important part of the healing process, as it helps individuals to reclaim their own sense of self and to assert control over their lives.

There are several types of boundaries that can be helpful for individuals who are healing from gaslighting. Physical boundaries involve setting limits on physical touch and proximity, and may include things like respecting personal space or setting rules about when and how physical contact is acceptable. Emotional boundaries involve setting limits on how much of one's own emotions and personal information are shared with others, and may include things like setting limits on how much emotional support is given or received. Mental boundaries involve setting limits on what information and ideas one is willing to accept or consider, and may include things like setting limits on how much time is spent engaging in certain activities or with certain people.

Setting boundaries can be a challenging process, especially for individuals who have experienced gaslighting or other forms of abuse. It may be difficult to assert control over one's own life and to set limits with manipulators or abusers. However, it is important to remember that setting boundaries is an important part of the healing process, and that it is possible to learn healthy ways of interacting with others.

There are several ways in which individuals can set and enforce boundaries in their relationships. One of the most effective ways is to communicate openly and honestly with others about what is and is not acceptable. This may involve setting clear limits and expectations, and being firm and assertive when these limits are crossed. It is also important to be consistent in enforcing boundaries, and to follow through with any consequences that may be necessary if boundaries are not respected.

Another important aspect of setting boundaries is learning to say "no" when necessary. This may involve setting limits on how much time or energy is given to others, or saying "no" to requests or demands that are not in one's own best interests. It is important to remember that it is okay to prioritize one's own needs and to set limits on how much time and energy is given to others.

It is also important for individuals who are healing from gaslighting to seek support from trusted friends, family members, or a mental health professional. These individuals can provide a sense of grounding and can help individuals to validate their own perceptions and experiences. It can also be helpful to seek out a support group or therapy, where individuals can connect with others who have experienced similar abuse and can learn healthy coping strategies.

In conclusion, boundaries play an important role in the healing process for individuals who have experienced gaslighting or other forms of abuse. Setting and enforcing boundaries can help individuals to reclaim their own sense of self and to assert control over their lives. It is important to communicate openly and honestly with others, to be consistent in enforcing boundaries, and to seek support from trusted individuals in order to learn healthy ways of interacting with others.

It is important for individuals who are healing from gaslighting to be mindful of their own mental health and to seek help if needed. The effects of gaslighting can be severe and long-lasting, and it is important to address any mental health issues that may arise as a result of the abuse. This may include seeking therapy or counseling, joining a support group, or seeking help from a mental health professional.

It is also important for individuals who are healing from gaslighting to practice self-care and to engage in activities that promote their own well-being. This may include exercising, engaging in hobbies, or seeking out activities that bring them joy and fulfillment. Taking care of oneself can help to build resilience and to provide a sense of stability and purpose, which can be especially important during times of uncertainty and stress.

It is also important for individuals who are healing from gaslighting to be mindful of their relationships and to surround themselves with supportive and caring individuals. This may involve seeking out new friendships or building healthier relationships with existing friends and family members. It may also be necessary to set boundaries with individuals who are not supportive or who engage in manipulative or abusive behaviors.

Healing from gaslighting can be a challenging and difficult process, but it is possible with the right support and resources. It is important to remember that no one deserves to be subjected to gaslighting or any other form of abuse, and that it is never too late to seek help and make positive changes in one's life. By seeking support and learning healthy coping strategies, individuals who have experienced gaslighting can break free from the cycle of abuse and reclaim their sense of self and reality.

It is also important for individuals who are healing from gaslighting to be aware of the potential triggers that may cause them to feel vulnerable or uncertain. Triggers may include certain people, places, or situations that remind the individual of the abuse they experienced. By being aware of these triggers, individuals can take steps to protect themselves and to maintain their own sense of stability and well-being.

One way to cope with triggers is to develop a plan for how to respond when they occur. This may involve seeking support from trusted friends or family members, practicing self-care activities, or seeking out a safe and supportive environment. It may also be helpful to talk through the trigger with a therapist or counselor, in order to better understand and manage the feelings that are associated with it.

It is also important for individuals who are healing from gaslighting to work on rebuilding their sense of self and trust in their own perceptions and instincts. This may involve seeking therapy or counseling, joining a support

group, or engaging in activities that promote self-awareness
and self-esteem. It is also important to remember that healing is a process and that it is okay to take things one step at
a time.

In conclusion, healing from gaslighting is a process that requires time, patience, and support. By setting boundaries,
seeking support, practicing self-care, and being aware of
triggers, individuals who have experienced gaslighting can
work towards rebuilding their sense of self and trust in their
own perceptions and instincts. It is important to remember
that no one deserves to be subjected to gaslighting or any
other form of abuse, and that it is never too late to seek help
and make positive changes in one's life.

06: The Importance of a Support System

Having a support system is an important aspect of mental health and well-being, and can be especially crucial for individuals who have experienced trauma or abuse. A support system can provide a sense of connection and belonging, and can offer emotional, practical, and social support. It can help individuals to feel less isolated and alone, and can provide a sense of hope and resilience during difficult times.

There are many different types of support systems, and what works best for one person may not be the same for another. Some people may find support through friends and family, while others may find it through professional support networks such as therapy or counseling. It is important for individuals to identify what types of support work best for them, and to build a support system that meets their needs.

One of the most important aspects of a support system is the ability to provide emotional support. This may involve listening to and validating an individual's experiences, offering words of encouragement or comfort, or simply being present for them during difficult times. Emotional support can help individuals to feel less alone and to cope with difficult emotions, and can be an important factor in helping them to heal and move forward.

Practical support can also be an important aspect of a support system. This may involve providing assistance with tasks such as grocery shopping or running errands, or offering financial or other resources. Practical support can help individuals to feel more secure and less overwhelmed, and can make a significant difference in their daily lives.

Social support is another important aspect of a support system. This may involve engaging in activities or hobbies with friends or family, or simply spending time together in a supportive and caring environment. Social support can help individuals to feel less isolated and more connected to others, and can provide a sense of meaning and purpose.

Having a support system is not always easy, and it may take time and effort to build a network of supportive relationships.

There are several steps that individuals can take to build a support system:

06: THE IMPORTANCE OF A SUPPORT SYSTEM

– Identify what types of support are most important to you: This may include emotional, practical, or social support, or a combination of all three. It is important to be honest with yourself about what you need and to seek out support that meets those needs.

– Reach out to others: It can be intimidating to ask for help, but it is important to remember that most people are willing to offer support if asked. Reach out to friends, family, or professionals and let them know what you need. It may also be helpful to join a support group or to seek out other resources such as therapy or counseling.

– Be open and honest: In order to receive support, it is important to be open and honest about your needs and feelings. This may involve sharing your experiences, talking about your emotions, or simply expressing a need for support. By being open and honest, you can build deeper and more meaningful relationships with others.

– Be willing to accept and give support: Support is a two-way street, and it is important to be willing to both give and receive support. This may involve offering practical or emotional support to others, or simply being present and available when needed. It is also important to be willing to accept support when it is offered, and to be open to trying new things or seeking help when needed.

– Take care of yourself: Building a support system is an important aspect of self-care, but it is not the only aspect. It is important to engage in activities that promote your own well-being, such as exercising, eating a healthy diet, and getting enough sleep. By taking care of yourself, you can build resilience and be better equipped to handle challenges and setbacks.

In conclusion, having a support system is an important aspect of mental health and well-being. It can provide a sense of connection and belonging, and can offer emotional, practical, and social support. There are many different types of support systems, and it is important for individuals to identify what works best for them and to build a support system that meets their needs. By reaching out to others, being open and honest, being willing to give and receive support, and taking care of themselves, individuals can build a strong and supportive network of relationships.

It is important to remember that building a support system

is a process, and that it may take time and effort to develop meaningful relationships. It is also important to be patient with yourself and to recognize that it is okay to take things one step at a time. Building a support system is not always easy, and it may involve facing challenges or setbacks along the way. However, with patience and persistence, it is possible to build a strong and supportive network of relationships that can provide a sense of connection, belonging, and hope during difficult times.

It is also important to be mindful of your own needs and boundaries when building a support system. It is okay to set limits on what you are willing and able to give, and to prioritize your own well-being. It is also important to be aware of any patterns of unhealthy or manipulative behavior in your relationships, and to set boundaries with individuals who are not supportive or who engage in abusive or manipulative behaviors.

Finally, it is important to remember that it is okay to seek help if you are struggling to build a support system or to cope with difficult emotions or experiences. Seeking help from a mental health professional or joining a support group can be an important step in the healing process, and can provide valuable resources and support.

In conclusion, the importance of a support system cannot be overstated. It can provide a sense of connection and belonging, and can offer emotional, practical, and social support. Building a support system is a process that may take time and effort, but with patience and persistence, it is possible to develop meaningful and supportive relationships. It is also important to be mindful of your own needs and boundaries, and to seek help if needed. By building a strong and supportive network of relationships, individuals can find hope and resilience during difficult times.

07: The Role of Counseling in Healing from Psychological Abuse

Counseling can be an important tool for individuals who are seeking to heal from psychological abuse. Psychological abuse, also known as emotional abuse or mental abuse, is a pattern of behavior that seeks to undermine an individual's sense of self-worth and confidence. It can involve things like manipulation, coercion, blame, criticism, or isolation, and can have serious and long-lasting effects on an individual's mental health and well-being.

Counseling can provide a safe and supportive environment for individuals to explore their experiences and emotions, and to work through the impact of abuse on their lives. It can also provide a space for individuals to learn healthy coping strategies and to develop a stronger sense of self and self-worth.

There are several ways in which counseling can be helpful for individuals who are healing from psychological abuse:

– Providing a safe and supportive environment: Counseling provides a space where individuals can feel safe and supported as they explore their experiences and emotions. This can be especially important for individuals who have experienced abuse, as it can help to build a sense of trust and openness that is necessary for healing.

– Validating experiences and emotions: Counseling can provide a space for individuals to have their experiences and emotions validated. This can be especially important for individuals who have experienced abuse, as they may feel that their feelings and perspectives are not being respected or understood. Validating an individual's experiences and emotions can help to build a sense of trust and can be an important step in the healing process.

– Exploring coping strategies: Counseling can provide a space for individuals to explore different coping strategies and to find what works best for them. This may involve learning new skills such as stress management or communication, or finding healthy ways to manage difficult emotions. Counseling can help individuals to develop a toolkit of coping strategies that they can draw upon in times of stress or hardship.

– Building self-worth and confidence: Counseling can help individuals to rebuild their sense of self-worth and confidence, which can be particularly important for those who have experienced abuse. Counseling can provide a space for individuals to work through any negative beliefs or self-doubt that may have been instilled by the abuser, and to develop a stronger sense of self and self-worth.

– Providing support and guidance: Counseling can provide ongoing support and guidance as individuals navigate the healing process. This can be especially helpful for individuals who are struggling to cope with the aftermath of abuse, and may feel overwhelmed or uncertain about what to do next. Counseling can provide a sense of direction and can help individuals to feel less alone and isolated as they work towards healing and recovery.

There are several different types of counseling that may be helpful for individuals who are healing from psychological abuse. Some common approaches include cognitive-behavioral therapy (CBT), dialectical behavior therapy (DBT), and trauma-focused therapy. These approaches may involve learning new coping strategies, exploring one's thoughts and feelings, or working through traumatic experiences in a safe and supportive environment. It is important for individuals to find a therapist who is trained in working with individuals who have experienced abuse, and who is able to provide the support and guidance that is needed.

It is important to remember that healing from psychological abuse is a process, and that it may take time and effort. Counseling can be an important tool in this process, and can provide a safe and supportive environment for individuals to explore their experiences and emotions, and to develop healthy coping strategies. By seeking counseling and support, individuals can work towards healing and recovery, and can build a stronger sense of self and self-worth.

It is also important for individuals who are seeking counseling to be patient with themselves and to recognize that healing is a process that may involve setbacks and challenges. It is important to be kind to oneself and to take things one step at a time. It is also important to be open to trying new things and to seeking additional support if needed.

It is also important for individuals who are seeking counseling to be aware of their own needs and boundaries, and to communicate these to their therapist. This may involve setting limits on the types of topics that are discussed, or setting boundaries around the amount of time and energy that is given to the therapy process. It is important to remember that it is okay to prioritize one's own well-being and to set limits when needed.

In conclusion, counseling can be an important tool for individuals who are seeking to heal from psychological abuse. It can provide a safe and supportive environment for individuals to explore their experiences and emotions, and to develop healthy coping strategies. By seeking counseling and support, individuals can work towards healing and recovery, and can build a stronger sense of self and self-worth. It is important to be patient with oneself, to be open to trying new things, and to be aware of one's own needs and boundaries in the therapy process.

08: The Process of Empowerment After Gaslighting

Empowerment is the process of regaining control over one's own life and well-being, and can be an important step in the healing process after experiencing gaslighting. Gaslighting is a form of psychological abuse that involves manipulating an individual's sense of reality, often in order to exert control over them. It can involve things like denying events or experiences, manipulating information, or causing the individual to doubt their own perceptions and memories. Gaslighting can have serious and long-lasting effects on an individual's mental health and well-being, and can make it difficult for them to trust their own thoughts and feelings.

The process of empowerment after gaslighting involves reclaiming one's own sense of self and reality, and rebuilding a sense of trust in oneself and one's own perceptions. It may involve seeking out support and resources, setting boundaries, and developing healthy coping strategies. Empowerment is a process that may take time and effort, but with patience and persistence, it is possible to regain control over one's own life and to move forward in a positive direction.

There are several steps that individuals can take to begin

08: THE PROCESS OF EMPOWERMENT AFTER GAS-LIGHTING

the process of empowerment after experiencing gaslighting:

– Seek out support and resources: It is important for individuals who are healing from gaslighting to seek out support and resources that can help them to rebuild their sense of self and trust in their own perceptions. This may involve seeking therapy or counseling, joining a support group, or seeking help from a trusted friend or family member.

– Set boundaries: Setting boundaries is an important aspect of empowerment after experiencing gaslighting. This may involve setting limits on the types of interactions or behaviors that are acceptable, or setting limits on the amount of time and energy that is given to certain relationships or activities. Setting boundaries can help individuals to protect their own well-being and to feel more in control of their own lives.

– Develop healthy coping strategies: Developing healthy coping strategies can be an important step in the process of empowerment after gaslighting. This may involve learning new skills such as stress management or communication, or finding healthy ways to manage difficult emotions. It may also involve finding activities or hobbies that bring joy and fulfillment, and that help to build a sense of purpose and meaning.

– Rebuild trust in oneself: Rebuilding trust in oneself can be a challenging but important aspect of the empowerment process after experiencing gaslighting. This may involve challenging negative beliefs or self-doubt that may have been instilled by the abuser, and rebuilding a sense of self-worth and confidence. It may also involve finding ways to validate one's own experiences and emotions, and to trust in one's own perceptions and instincts.

Empowerment after gaslighting is a process that may involve challenges and setbacks, but with patience and persistence, it is possible to reclaim control over one's own life and to move forward in a positive direction. It is important to be kind to oneself and to recognize that healing is a process that may take time. By seeking out support and resources, setting boundaries, developing healthy coping strategies, and rebuilding trust in oneself, individuals can work towards empowerment and recovery after experiencing gaslighting.

It is also important for individuals who are working towards empowerment after gaslighting to be mindful of their own needs and boundaries, and to prioritize their own well-being. This may involve taking breaks or setting limits on certain activities or relationships, or seeking additional support if needed. It is important to remember that it is okay to put one's own needs first and to prioritize self-care.

It is also important to be aware of any potential triggers that may arise during the empowerment process. Triggers are things that may remind an individual of the abuse they experienced, and can cause them to feel vulnerable or uncertain. By being aware of these triggers, individuals can take steps to protect themselves and to maintain their own sense of stability and well-being.

In conclusion, the process of empowerment after gaslighting involves reclaiming control over one's own life and well-being, and rebuilding a sense of trust in oneself and one's own perceptions. It may involve seeking out support and resources, setting boundaries, and developing healthy coping strategies. Empowerment is a process that may take time and effort, but with patience and persistence, it is possible to move forward in a positive direction. It is important to be mindful of one's own needs and boundaries, and to be aware of any potential triggers that may arise during the empowerment process. By taking these steps, individuals can work towards empowerment and recovery after experiencing gaslighting.

It is important to remember that the process of empowerment after gaslighting is unique to each individual, and what works for one person may not be the same for another. It is important for individuals to be patient with themselves and to recognize that healing is a process that may involve setbacks and challenges. It is also important to be open to trying new things and to seeking additional support if needed.

It is also important to be aware of any patterns of unhealthy or abusive behavior in one's relationships, and to set boundaries with individuals who are not supportive or who engage in abusive or manipulative behaviors. This may involve seeking therapy or counseling, or seeking help from a trusted friend or family member. By setting boundaries and seeking support, individuals can work towards building healthy and supportive relationships that are based on respect and trust.

It is also important for individuals who are working towards empowerment after gaslighting to be mindful of their own self-care and well-being. This may involve engaging in activities that promote physical and emotional health, such as exercising, eating a healthy diet, and getting enough sleep. By taking care of oneself, individuals can build resilience and be better equipped to handle challenges and setbacks.

In conclusion, the process of empowerment after gaslighting is a unique and individualized process that involves reclaiming control over one's own life and well-being, and rebuilding a sense of trust in oneself and one's own perceptions. It may involve seeking out support and resources, setting boundaries, and developing healthy coping strategies. By being patient with oneself, open to trying new things, and mindful of one's own self-care and well-being, individuals can work towards empowerment and recovery after experiencing gaslighting.

09: Rediscovering Your Worth and Building Self-Esteem

Rediscovering one's worth and building self-esteem are important steps in the process of personal growth and development. Self-esteem is defined as an individual's overall sense of self-worth and confidence, and is an important aspect of mental health and well-being. When we have healthy self-esteem, we are more likely to feel confident and capable, and to take risks and pursue our goals. When our self-esteem is low, we may feel uncertain or unworthy, and may struggle to take care of ourselves or to set healthy boundaries.

Rediscovering one's worth and building self-esteem can be a challenging but rewarding process, and may involve exploring one's own values, setting goals, and learning new skills. It is important to be patient with oneself and to recognize that building self-esteem is a process that may take time and effort.

There are several steps that individuals can take to rediscover their worth and build self-esteem:

– Explore your values: One of the first steps in rediscovering your worth and building self-esteem is to explore your own values and beliefs. This may involve asking yourself questions such as "What is important to me?", "What are my goals and aspirations?", and "What makes me feel fulfilled and satisfied?" By exploring your own values, you can begin to understand what is most important to you and to build a sense of purpose and direction in your life.

– Set goals: Setting goals is an important aspect of building self-esteem, as it provides a sense of direction and helps to focus our energy and efforts. Goals can be short-term or long-term, and can be related to various areas of our lives such as career, relationships, personal growth, or health and wellness. By setting goals and working towards their achievement, we can build a sense of accomplishment and self-worth.

– Learn new skills: Learning new skills is a great way to build self-esteem and to feel more confident and capable. This may involve learning a new hobby or skill, or pursuing education or training in a particular area. By challenging ourselves and expanding our knowledge and abilities, we can build self-esteem and feel more confident in our own abilities.

– Practice self-care: Taking care of ourselves is an important aspect of building self-esteem, as it helps us to feel more capable and in control of our lives. Self-care can involve things like exercising, eating a healthy diet, getting enough sleep, and taking time for relaxation and leisure. By taking care of ourselves, we can build resilience and feel more capable of handling challenges and setbacks.

– Seek support and resources: Seeking support and resources can be an important aspect of building self-esteem, especially if we are struggling with low self-esteem or self-doubt. This may involve seeking therapy or counseling, joining a support group, or seeking help from a trusted friend or family member. By seeking support and resources, we can gain valuable perspective and guidance, and can build a stronger sense of self-worth and confidence.

– Set boundaries: Setting boundaries is an important aspect of building self-esteem, as it helps us to protect our own well-being and to feel more in control of our lives. Boundaries can be physical, emotional, or mental, and may involve setting limits on the types of interactions or behaviors that are acceptable, or setting limits on the amount of time and energy that is given to certain relationships or activities. By setting boundaries, we can feel more in control of our own lives and more able to take care of ourselves.

– Practice gratitude: Practicing gratitude is a simple but powerful way to build self-esteem and to feel more positive and hopeful. This may involve keeping a gratitude journal or making a list of things that we are thankful for each day. By focusing on the things that are going well in our lives, we can build a sense of appreciation and positivity, and can feel more confident and capable.

– Seek positive role models: Seeking positive role models can be a helpful way to build self-esteem and to gain perspective on what is possible. This may involve finding individuals who inspire us or who have achieved success in areas that are important to us. By seeking positive role models, we can gain insight and inspiration, and can feel more motivated and capable of achieving our own goals.

In conclusion, rediscovering one's worth and building self-esteem are important steps in the process of personal growth and development. It is a process that may take time and effort, and may involve exploring one's values, setting goals, learning new skills, practicing self-care, seeking support and resources, setting boundaries, practicing gratitude, and seeking positive role models. By taking these steps, individuals can build a stronger sense of self-worth and confidence, and can feel more capable and in control of their own lives.

It is important to remember that building self-esteem is a process that may involve challenges and setbacks, and it is important to be patient with oneself and to recognize that it is a journey. It is also important to be kind to oneself and to recognize that we are all human and that it is okay to make mistakes. By practicing self-compassion and by focusing on our strengths and accomplishments, we can build self-esteem and feel more positive and confident.

It is also important to be aware of negative self-talk and to challenge negative beliefs or thoughts that may be hindering our self-esteem. Negative self-talk can be damaging to our self-esteem and can hold us back from achieving our goals. By recognizing and challenging negative self-talk, we can build a stronger sense of self-worth and confidence.

It is also important to be open to seeking support and resources if needed. This may involve seeking therapy or counseling, joining a support group, or seeking help from a trusted friend or family member. By seeking support, we can gain valuable perspective and guidance, and can build a stronger sense of self-worth and confidence.

In conclusion, building self-esteem is a process that involves exploring one's values, setting goals, learning new skills, practicing self-care, seeking support and resources, setting boundaries, practicing gratitude, and seeking positive role models. It is a process that may involve challenges and setbacks, and it is important to be patient with oneself and to recognize that it is a journey. By being kind to oneself, recognizing and challenging negative self-talk, and seeking support and resources if needed, individuals can build self-esteem and feel more positive and confident.

10: The Role of Self-Care in the Healing Process

Self-care is an important aspect of the healing process, and involves taking care of one's own physical, emotional, and mental well-being. It is a necessary and vital aspect of self-care that can help individuals to feel more balanced, grounded, and resilient. When we practice self-care, we are better equipped to cope with the challenges and stresses of life, and to make positive choices for ourselves.

There are many different forms of self-care, and what works for one person may not be the same for another. Some common forms of self-care include:

Exercise and physical activity: Exercise and physical activity are important forms of self-care that can help to reduce stress, improve sleep, and boost mood. This may involve engaging in activities such as walking, running, swimming, or yoga.

Eating a healthy diet: A healthy diet is an important aspect of self-care, as it can help to support physical and mental well-being. This may involve incorporating a variety of nutrients and whole foods into one's diet, and avoiding processed or unhealthy foods.

Getting enough sleep: Sleep is an important form of self-care, as it is essential for physical and mental health. It is important to aim for 7-9 hours of sleep each night, and to create a sleep-friendly environment that is conducive to rest.

Taking breaks and relaxation: Taking breaks and relaxation are important forms of self-care that can help to reduce stress and improve well-being. This may involve activities such as reading, watching a movie, or taking a relaxing bath.

Seeking social support: Social support is an important form of self-care, as it can help to reduce feelings of isolation and loneliness, and can provide a sense of connection and belonging. This may involve seeking out supportive friends and family members, or joining a support group.

Practicing mindfulness: Mindfulness is a form of self-care that involves bringing one's attention to the present moment, and can help to reduce stress and improve well-being. This may involve activities such as meditation, deep breathing, or journaling.

By incorporating self-care activities into our lives, we can support our own healing and well-being, and feel more balanced and resilient. It is important to recognize that self-care is a necessary and vital aspect of our overall well-

being, and to prioritize it in our daily lives. It is also important to remember that self-care is not selfish, but rather it is an essential aspect of taking care of ourselves and being able to give back to others.

Self-care is particularly important during the healing process, as it can help to reduce stress and improve well-being. When we are healing from a difficult or traumatic experience, it is common to feel overwhelmed, exhausted, or drained. Self-care can help to nourish and restore us, and can provide a sense of comfort and support. It can also help to reduce feelings of anxiety or depression, and can improve our overall sense of well-being.

There are several steps that individuals can take to prioritize self-care during the healing process:

10: THE ROLE OF SELF-CARE IN THE HEALING PROCESS

– Identify your needs: The first step in prioritizing self-care during the healing process is to identify your own needs and what forms of self-care are most helpful for you. This may involve exploring your own values and what brings you joy and fulfillment, or seeking guidance from a therapist or other trusted resource.

– Set boundaries: Setting boundaries is an important aspect of self-care, as it helps to protect our own well-being and to feel more in control of our lives. Boundaries can be physical, emotional, or mental, and may involve setting limits on the types of interactions or behaviors that are acceptable, or setting limits on the amount of time and energy that is given to certain relationships or activities. By setting boundaries, we can feel more in control of our own lives and more able to take care of ourselves.

– Make self-care a priority: Once you have identified your needs and set boundaries, it is important to make self-care a priority in your daily life. This may involve setting aside dedicated time for self-care activities, or incorporating self-care into your daily routine. It is also important to be mindful of your own self-care needs and to prioritize them in your daily life.

– Seek support: Seeking support is an important aspect of self-care, and can be especially helpful during the healing process. This may involve seeking therapy or counseling, joining a support group, or seeking help from a trusted friend or family member. By seeking support, we can gain valuable perspective and guidance, and can feel more connected and less alone.

In conclusion, self-care is an important aspect of the healing process, and involves taking care of one's own physical, emotional, and mental well-being. By incorporating self-care activities into our lives, we can support our own healing and well-being, and feel more balanced and resilient. It is important to prioritize self-care, set boundaries, and seek support during the healing process. By taking these steps, individuals can further support their healing journey and improve their overall sense of well-being.

It is important to recognize that self-care looks different for everyone, and what works for one person may not be the same for another. It is important to be mindful of your own needs and to experiment with different forms of self-care to see what works best for you. It is also important to be kind to yourself and to recognize that it is okay to take breaks and to set limits when needed.

It is also important to be aware of any patterns of unhealthy or self-defeating behavior, and to seek help if needed. This may involve seeking therapy or counseling, or seeking help from a trusted friend or family member. By seeking help and support, individuals can work towards building healthy and supportive relationships that are based on respect and trust.

In conclusion, self-care is an important aspect of the healing process, and involves taking care of one's own physical, emotional, and mental well-being. It is a necessary and vital aspect of self-care that can help individuals to feel more balanced, grounded, and resilient. By incorporating self-care activities into our lives, setting boundaries, and seeking support, individuals can further support their healing journey and improve their overall sense of well-being.

11: Navigating Life After Gaslighting: Tips for Moving Forward

Navigating life after gaslighting can be a challenging and difficult process, as it involves rebuilding trust in oneself and one's own perceptions, and reclaiming control over one's own life and well-being. It is a process that may take time and effort, but with patience and persistence, it is possible to move forward in a positive direction.

There are several steps that individuals can take to navigate life after gaslighting and to move forward:

– Seek support: Seeking support is an important aspect of navigating life after gaslighting, as it can provide a sense of connection and belonging, and can help to reduce feelings of isolation and loneliness. This may involve seeking therapy or counseling, joining a support group, or seeking help from a trusted friend or family member. By seeking support, individuals can gain valuable perspective and guidance, and can feel more connected and less alone.

– Set boundaries: Setting boundaries is an important aspect of navigating life after gaslighting, as it helps to protect one's own well-being and to feel more in control of one's own life. Boundaries can be physical, emotional, or mental, and may involve setting limits on the types of interactions or behaviors that are acceptable, or setting limits on the amount of time and energy that is given to certain relationships or activities. By setting boundaries, individuals can feel more in control of their own lives and more able to take care of themselves.

– Practice self-care: Practicing self-care is an important aspect of navigating life after gaslighting, as it helps to reduce stress and improve well-being. Self-care can involve activities such as exercise, eating a healthy diet, getting enough sleep, and taking time for relaxation and leisure. By taking care of oneself, individuals can build resilience and feel more capable of handling challenges and setbacks.

– Learn to trust oneself: Trusting oneself is an important aspect of navigating life after gaslighting, as it involves rebuilding trust in one's own perceptions and experiences. This may involve learning to recognize and challenge negative self-talk, and working to develop a sense of self-acceptance and self-compassion. It is important to be patient with oneself and to recognize that rebuilding trust in oneself is a process that may take time.

– Seek out positive influences: Seeking out positive influences is an important aspect of navigating life after gaslighting, as it can help to provide a sense of support and encouragement. This may involve seeking out positive role models or seeking out supportive friends and family members. By seeking out positive influences, individuals can gain insight and inspiration, and can feel more motivated and supported.

– Set goals: Setting goals is an important aspect of navigating life after gaslighting, as it provides a sense of direction and helps to focus energy and efforts. Goals can be short-term or long-term, and can be related to various areas of one's life such as career, relationships, personal growth, or health and wellness. By setting goals and working towards their achievement, individuals can build a sense of accomplishment and self-worth.

In conclusion, navigating life after gaslighting can be a challenging and difficult process, but with patience and persistence, it is possible to move forward in a positive direction. By seeking support, setting boundaries, practicing self-care, learning to trust oneself, seeking out positive influences, and setting goals, individuals can navigate life after gaslighting and work towards rebuilding trust in oneself and reclaiming control over one's own life and well-being.

It is important to recognize that navigating life after gaslighting is a process that may involve challenges and setbacks, and it is important to be patient with oneself and to recognize that it is a journey. It is also important to be kind to oneself and to recognize that we are all human and that it is okay to make mistakes. By practicing self-compassion and by focusing on our strengths and accomplishments, we can build self-esteem and feel more positive and confident.

It is also important to be aware of negative self-talk and to challenge negative beliefs or thoughts that may be hindering our progress. Negative self-talk can be damaging to our self-esteem and can hold us back from achieving our goals. By recognizing and challenging negative self-talk, we can build a stronger sense of self-worth and confidence.

It is also important to be open to seeking support and resources if needed. This may involve seeking therapy or counseling, joining a support group, or seeking help from a trusted friend or family member. By seeking support, we can gain valuable perspective and guidance, and can build a stronger sense of self-worth and confidence.

In conclusion, navigating life after gaslighting is a process that involves seeking support, setting boundaries, practicing self-care, learning to trust oneself, seeking out positive influences, and setting goals. It is a process that may involve challenges and setbacks, and it is important to be patient with oneself and to recognize that it is a journey. By being kind to oneself, recognizing and challenging negative self-talk, and seeking support and resources if needed, individuals can navigate life after gaslighting and work towards rebuilding trust in oneself and reclaiming control over one's own life and well-being.

12: The Importance of Self-Compassion in Healing from Psychological Abuse

Self-compassion is an important aspect of healing from psychological abuse, as it involves treating oneself with kindness, understanding, and care, and recognizing that we are all human and that we all make mistakes. It is a powerful tool that can help individuals to heal from psychological abuse and to build a stronger sense of self-worth and confidence.

Self-compassion involves three core components: self-kindness, common humanity, and mindfulness.

– Self-kindness involves treating oneself with kindness and understanding, rather than with judgment or criticism. It involves being gentle and caring towards oneself, and recognizing that we all have flaws and limitations.

– Common humanity involves recognizing that suffering and struggles are a common part of the human experience, and that we are not alone in our experiences. It involves recognizing that we are all connected and that we all experience difficult emotions and challenges.

12: THE IMPORTANCE OF SELF-COMPASSION IN HEALING FROM PSYCHOLOGICAL ABUSE

– Mindfulness involves bringing awareness to the present moment and to our own thoughts and emotions without judgment. It involves accepting our experiences and emotions as they are, rather than trying to avoid or suppress them.

Self-compassion can be a powerful tool in healing from psychological abuse, as it helps to reduce feelings of shame and self-blame, and can help individuals to feel more accepting and understanding towards themselves. It can also help to reduce feelings of anxiety and depression, and can improve overall well-being.

There are several ways that individuals can practice self-compassion:

– Practice self-kindness: This may involve speaking to oneself in a kind and caring manner, or engaging in activities that bring joy and fulfillment.

– Remember that we are all human: This may involve reminding oneself that it is okay to make mistakes, and that we all have flaws and limitations.

12: THE IMPORTANCE OF SELF-COMPASSION IN HEALING FROM PSYCHOLOGICAL ABUSE

– Practice mindfulness: This may involve activities such as meditation, deep breathing, or journaling.

– Seek support: This may involve seeking therapy or counseling, joining a support group, or seeking help from a trusted friend or family member.

By practicing self-compassion, individuals can build a stronger sense of self-worth and confidence, and can feel more accepting and understanding towards themselves. It is an important aspect of healing from psychological abuse, and can help individuals to feel more resilient and capable of coping with challenges and setbacks.

It is important to recognize that practicing self-compassion is a process that may involve challenges and setbacks, and it is important to be patient with oneself and to recognize that it is a journey. It is also important to be kind to oneself and to recognize that we are all human and that it is okay to make mistakes. By focusing on our strengths and accomplishments, and by seeking support and resources if needed, we can build self-compassion and feel more positive and confident.

12: THE IMPORTANCE OF SELF-COMPASSION IN HEALING FROM PSYCHOLOGICAL ABUSE

In conclusion, self-compassion is an important aspect of healing from psychological abuse, and involves treating oneself with kindness, understanding, and care, and recognizing that we are all human and that we all make mistakes. It is a powerful tool that can help individuals to heal from psychological abuse and to build a stronger sense of self-worth and confidence. By practicing self-compassion, individuals can feel more accepting and understanding towards themselves, and can build resilience and feel more capable of coping with challenges and setbacks.

It is important to recognize that healing from psychological abuse is a process that may involve challenges and setbacks, and it is important to be patient with oneself and to recognize that it is a journey. It is also important to be kind to oneself and to recognize that it is okay to take breaks and to set limits when needed. By practicing self-compassion and by seeking support and resources if needed, individuals can further support their healing journey and build resilience and well-being.

It is also important to be aware of any patterns of unhealthy or self-defeating behavior, and to seek help if needed. This may involve seeking therapy or counseling, or seeking help from a trusted friend or family member. By seeking help and support, individuals can work towards building healthy and supportive relationships that are based on respect and trust.

In conclusion, healing from psychological abuse is a process that involves practicing self-compassion, seeking support, and being aware of any patterns of unhealthy or self-defeating behavior. It is a process that may involve challenges and setbacks, and it is important to be patient with oneself and to recognize that it is a journey. By being kind to oneself, seeking support and resources if needed, and working towards building healthy and supportive relationships, individuals can further support their healing journey and build resilience and well-being.

13: Finding Hope and Resilience After Gaslighting

Finding hope and resilience after gaslighting can be a challenging and difficult process, as it involves rebuilding trust in oneself and one's own perceptions, and reclaiming control over one's own life and well-being. It is a process that may take time and effort, but with patience and persistence, it is possible to find hope and resilience and to move forward in a positive direction.

There are several steps that individuals can take to find hope and resilience after gaslighting:

– Seek support: Seeking support is an important aspect of finding hope and resilience after gaslighting, as it can provide a sense of connection and belonging, and can help to reduce feelings of isolation and loneliness. This may involve seeking therapy or counseling, joining a support group, or seeking help from a trusted friend or family member. By seeking support, individuals can gain valuable perspective and guidance, and can feel more connected and less alone.

– Set boundaries: Setting boundaries is an important aspect

of finding hope and resilience after gaslighting, as it helps to protect one's own well-being and to feel more in control of one's own life. Boundaries can be physical, emotional, or mental, and may involve setting limits on the types of interactions or behaviors that are acceptable, or setting limits on the amount of time and energy that is given to certain relationships or activities. By setting boundaries, individuals can feel more in control of their own lives and more able to take care of themselves.

– Practice self-care: Practicing self-care is an important aspect of finding hope and resilience after gaslighting, as it helps to reduce stress and improve well-being. Self-care can involve activities such as exercise, eating a healthy diet, getting enough sleep, and taking time for relaxation and leisure. By taking care of oneself, individuals can build resilience and feel more capable of handling challenges and setbacks.

– Learn to trust oneself: Trusting oneself is an important aspect of finding hope and resilience after gaslighting, as it involves rebuilding trust in one's own perceptions and experiences. This may involve learning to recognize and challenge negative self-talk, and working to develop a sense of self-acceptance and self-compassion. It is important to be patient with oneself and to recognize that rebuilding trust in oneself is a process that may take time.

– Seek out positive influences: Seeking out positive influences is an important aspect of finding hope and resilience after gaslighting, as it can help to provide a sense of support and encouragement. This may involve seeking out positive role models or seeking out supportive friends and family members. By seeking out positive influences, individuals can gain insight and inspiration, and can feel more motivated and supported.

In conclusion, finding hope and resilience after gaslighting is a process that involves seeking support, setting boundaries, practicing self-care, learning to trust oneself, and seeking out positive influences. It is a process that may involve challenges and setbacks, and it is important to be patient with oneself and to recognize that it is a journey. By taking these steps, individuals can find hope and resilience after gaslighting and work towards rebuilding trust in oneself and reclaiming control over one's own life and well-being.

13: FINDING HOPE AND RESILIENCE AFTER GAS-LIGHTING

It is important to recognize that finding hope and resilience after gaslighting is a process that may involve challenges and setbacks, and it is important to be patient with oneself and to recognize that it is a journey. It is also important to be kind to oneself and to recognize that we are all human and that it is okay to make mistakes. By focusing on our strengths and accomplishments, and by seeking support and resources if needed, we can build hope and resilience and feel more positive and confident.

It is also important to be aware of negative self-talk and to challenge negative beliefs or thoughts that may be hindering our progress. Negative self-talk can be damaging to our self-esteem and can hold us back from achieving our goals. By recognizing and challenging negative self-talk, we can build a stronger sense of hope and resilience.

It is also important to be open to seeking support and resources if needed. This may involve seeking therapy or counseling, joining a support group, or seeking help from a trusted friend or family member. By seeking support, we can gain valuable perspective and guidance, and can build a stronger sense of hope and resilience.

13: FINDING HOPE AND RESILIENCE AFTER GAS-LIGHTING

In conclusion, finding hope and resilience after gaslighting is a process that involves seeking support, setting boundaries, practicing self-care, learning to trust oneself, and seeking out positive influences. It is a process that may involve challenges and setbacks, and it is important to be patient with oneself and to recognize that it is a journey. By being kind to oneself, recognizing and challenging negative self-talk, and seeking support and resources if needed, individuals can find hope and resilience after gaslighting and work towards rebuilding trust in oneself and reclaiming control over one's own life and well-being.

One way to find hope and resilience after gaslighting is to focus on small steps and progress, rather than on the overall journey. This can help to break the process down into manageable chunks, and can help to provide a sense of accomplishment and progress. It is important to be patient with oneself and to recognize that healing is a process that may take time, and to celebrate small victories along the way.

It is also important to remember that it is okay to feel a range of emotions, including anger, sadness, and frustration, and to allow oneself to feel and process these emotions. By acknowledging and expressing these emotions, individuals can begin to heal and move forward.

It is also important to be mindful of self-care and to prioritize taking care of oneself. This may involve activities such as exercise, eating a healthy diet, getting enough sleep, and taking time for relaxation and leisure. By taking care of oneself, individuals can build resilience and feel more capable of handling challenges and setbacks.

In conclusion, finding hope and resilience after gaslighting is a process that involves seeking support, setting boundaries, practicing self-care, learning to trust oneself, and seeking out positive influences. It is a process that may involve challenges and setbacks, and it is important to be patient with oneself and to recognize that it is a journey. By focusing on small steps and progress, allowing oneself to feel and process a range of emotions, and prioritizing self-care, individuals can find hope and resilience after gaslighting and work towards rebuilding trust in oneself and reclaiming control over one's own life and well-being.

Book 2 - Narcissistic Abuse

A Deep Dive into the Psychodynamics of Narcissistic Personality Disorder and Its Effects on the Self-Esteem, Well-Being, and Emotional Health of Those Who Have Suffered from Its Toxic Influence

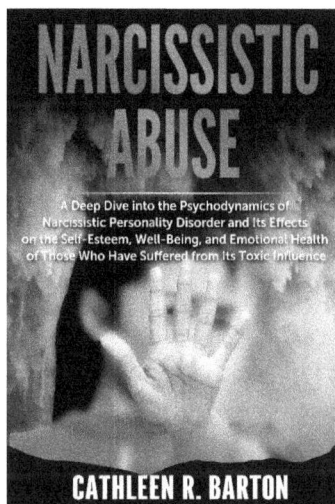

01: What is Narcissistic Personality Disorder?

Narcissistic Personality Disorder (NPD) is a mental health condition characterized by an inflated sense of self-importance and a deep need for admiration. People with NPD often have a grandiose sense of their own capabilities and accomplishments, and they expect to be recognized as superior without having to meet the same standards as others.

At the core of NPD is a fragile ego that is easily threatened and prone to feelings of inadequacy. To protect themselves from these vulnerabilities, individuals with NPD may engage in a range of behaviors designed to boost their own ego and draw attention to themselves. These behaviors can include grandiose displays of wealth or success, manipulation of others, and a lack of empathy towards the feelings and needs of others.

NPD is classified as a "Cluster B" personality disorder, which means that it is characterized by dramatic and erratic behavior. Other personality disorders in this category include Borderline Personality Disorder, Antisocial Personality Disorder, and Histrionic Personality Disorder.

01: WHAT IS NARCISSISTIC PERSONALITY DISORDER?

Symptoms of NPD can be difficult to identify, as people with the disorder often present a highly favorable image of themselves to the world. However, common signs of NPD may include:

– An exaggerated sense of self-importance

– A preoccupation with fantasies of unlimited success, power, or attractiveness

– A belief that they are special and should only associate with other special or high-status people

– A need for excessive admiration and attention

– A lack of empathy towards others' feelings and needs

– Envy of others and a belief that others are envious of them

– Arrogant and haughty behavior

It is important to note that having some of these traits does not necessarily mean that someone has NPD. To be diagnosed with the disorder, a person must exhibit a significant number of these traits and have a pattern of behavior that is significantly different from what is considered normal in their cultural context.

NPD is often accompanied by other mental health conditions, such as depression, anxiety, and substance abuse disorders. It is also more common in men than in women.

The exact cause of NPD is not fully understood, but it is thought to be the result of a combination of genetic, environmental, and social factors. Some research suggests that people who have experienced childhood abuse or neglect may be more at risk of developing NPD later in life.

Treatment for NPD typically involves a combination of psychotherapy and medication. Psychotherapy, such as cognitive-behavioral therapy (CBT), can help individuals with NPD learn to recognize and change their unhealthy patterns of thinking and behavior. Medications, such as selective serotonin reuptake inhibitors (SSRIs), may be used to treat any accompanying mental health conditions, such as depression or anxiety.

It is important to note that NPD can be a difficult condition to treat, as individuals with the disorder may not recognize that they have a problem and may resist treatment. It is also common for people with NPD to have difficulty maintaining relationships and may struggle with social isolation as a result of their behavior.

In conclusion, Narcissistic Personality Disorder is a mental health condition characterized by an inflated sense of self-importance and a deep need for admiration. It is characterized by a range of behaviors designed to boost the individual's ego and draw attention to themselves, and is often accompanied by other mental health conditions. While it can be a challenging condition to treat, a combination of psychotherapy and medication can be effective in helping individuals with NPD learn to recognize and change their unhealthy patterns of thinking and behavior.

It is important to recognize that not all narcissistic behavior is indicative of NPD. It is common for people to have some narcissistic traits, and it is only when these traits become extreme and dysfunctional that they may be indicative of a personality disorder.

It is also important to recognize that people with NPD are not necessarily "bad" or malevolent. Many people with NPD may not be aware of the impact their behavior has on others and may not understand the pain and suffering they cause. With proper treatment, individuals with NPD can learn to recognize and change their unhealthy patterns of behavior and develop healthier, more fulfilling relationships.

It is also important for loved ones of individuals with NPD to seek support and take care of their own well-being. Dealing with someone with NPD can be emotionally draining and can take a toll on one's own mental health. It is important to set boundaries, practice self-care, and seek support from friends, family, or a therapist if needed.

In summary, Narcissistic Personality Disorder is a complex and often misunderstood mental health condition that can have a significant impact on the lives of those affected by it. It is important to recognize the signs of NPD and seek treatment if necessary in order to improve the well-being and relationships of those affected by the disorder.

It is also important for individuals who have experienced narcissistic abuse to seek support and seek help in healing from the trauma. Narcissistic abuse can have serious consequences for one's emotional well-being and can leave a person feeling confused, isolated, and lacking in self-worth.

01: WHAT IS NARCISSISTIC PERSONALITY DISORDER?

Therapy can be a helpful resource for individuals who have experienced narcissistic abuse, as it can provide a safe and supportive space to process and work through the trauma. It can also be helpful to join a support group or connect with others who have experienced similar abuse, as it can provide a sense of community and understanding.

It is also important to remember that healing from narcissistic abuse takes time, and it is important to be patient with oneself and to practice self-care. This can include activities such as exercise, meditation, and engaging in activities that bring joy and relaxation.

In conclusion, it is important to recognize the serious impact that narcissistic abuse can have on one's emotional health and well-being. It is important to seek support and treatment in order to heal from the trauma and build a healthy and fulfilling life.

It is also important for individuals to educate themselves about narcissistic abuse and the dynamics of narcissistic relationships. Understanding the patterns of behavior and the tactics that narcissists use can help individuals recognize abusive behavior and take steps to protect themselves from it.

It is also important to remember that not all narcissists are the same, and the behaviors and tactics that they use can vary. Some narcissists may be more overt and aggressive in their abuse, while others may be more subtle and manipulative.

It is also important to recognize that not all relationships with narcissists have to be toxic. With proper boundaries, communication, and self-care, it is possible to have a relationship with a narcissist that is functional and healthy.

In conclusion, it is important for individuals to educate themselves about narcissistic abuse and to take steps to protect themselves from it. It is also important to recognize that healing from narcissistic abuse takes time and to be patient with oneself during the healing process. With proper support and treatment, it is possible to build a healthy and fulfilling life after experiencing narcissistic abuse.

02: The Characteristics of Narcissistic Abuse

Narcissistic abuse is a form of psychological abuse that is characterized by a pattern of manipulation, control, and exploitation in a relationship. It is often perpetrated by individuals with Narcissistic Personality Disorder (NPD), although not all narcissists engage in abusive behavior.

One of the defining characteristics of narcissistic abuse is that it is covert and insidious. Narcissists are often skilled at hiding their abusive behavior and may even present a charming and likable exterior to the world. This can make it difficult for victims of narcissistic abuse to recognize that they are being abused and to seek help.

There are a range of tactics that narcissists may use in order to maintain control and manipulate their victims. These tactics can include:

– Gaslighting: This refers to the act of manipulating someone into doubting their own perceptions and memories. A narcissist may deny that certain events occurred, or they may manipulate evidence in order to make their victim question their own recollection of events.

– Triangulation: This involves bringing a third party into the dynamic of the relationship in order to create jealousy and insecurity in the victim. A narcissist may flirt with other people in front of their victim or compare their victim to others in order to undermine their self-esteem.

– Love bombing: This involves showering the victim with excessive attention, affection, and gifts in the early stages of the relationship in order to create an intense bond. This can make it difficult for the victim to leave the relationship later on.

– Isolation: A narcissist may try to isolate their victim from friends and family in order to increase their dependence on the narcissist and to make it more difficult for the victim to seek support.

– Economic abuse: A narcissist may control their victim's access to financial resources in order to maintain control over the victim. This can include withholding money, controlling how the victim spends money, or preventing the victim from working.

– Emotional abuse: Narcissists may use a range of tactics to emotionally abuse their victims, including belittling, criticizing, and mocking their victim's feelings and needs. They may also use emotional blackmail in order to get their victim to do what they want, such as threatening to harm themselves if their victim does not comply.

– Physical abuse: While not all narcissists engage in physical abuse, some may use physical violence as a means of control. This can include hitting, pushing, or restraining their victim.

One of the most damaging aspects of narcissistic abuse is the way it can erode the victim's sense of self-worth and identity. Narcissists may use a range of tactics to chip away at their victim's self-esteem, including criticism, belittling, and manipulation. This can leave the victim feeling confused, isolated, and unsure of their own perceptions and feelings.

It is important to recognize that narcissistic abuse can have serious consequences for the mental health and well-being of the victim. It can lead to anxiety, depression, and post-traumatic stress disorder (PTSD). It is also common for victims of narcissistic abuse to develop a sense of learned helplessness, in which they feel unable to make decisions or take action on their own.

If you suspect that you or someone you know is experiencing narcissistic abuse, it is important to seek help. This can include talking to a therapist or counselor, reaching out to a support group, or contacting a domestic violence hotline for guidance and support.

In conclusion, narcissistic abuse is a form of psychological abuse that is characterized by a pattern of manipulation and control. It can have serious consequences for the mental health and well-being of the victim, and it is important to seek help if you suspect that you or someone you know is experiencing this type of abuse.

It is also important for individuals who have experienced narcissistic abuse to remember that they are not alone and that they are not to blame for the abuse they have suffered. It can be easy for victims of narcissistic abuse to internalize the blame and to believe that they are responsible for the abuse. It is important to recognize that the abuse is not the victim's fault and that they have the right to seek help and to create a healthy and fulfilling life for themselves.

It is also important for individuals who have experienced

narcissistic abuse to work on rebuilding their sense of self and their self-worth. This can be a difficult process, but it is an essential step in the healing journey. Therapy can be a helpful resource in this process, as can connecting with others who have experienced similar abuse.

It is also important to set boundaries and to learn to assert oneself in healthy ways. This can include learning how to say no, setting limits on what is acceptable behavior, and seeking support when needed.

In conclusion, recovering from narcissistic abuse is a process that takes time and effort. It is important to seek help, to work on rebuilding a sense of self, and to set boundaries in order to create a healthy and fulfilling life. With the right support and resources, it is possible to heal from the trauma of narcissistic abuse and to create a life that is fulfilling and satisfying.

It is also important for individuals who have experienced narcissistic abuse to remember that healing is a journey and that it is okay to take things one step at a time. It is important to be patient with oneself and to recognize that it is normal to have setbacks and difficult days.

It is also important to have self-compassion and to treat oneself with kindness and understanding. This can be especially difficult for individuals who have experienced narcissistic abuse, as their sense of self-worth may have been severely damaged. It is important to remind oneself that it is okay to make mistakes and that it is possible to learn from them and grow.

It is also important to focus on self-care and to prioritize one's own well-being. This can include activities such as exercise, meditation, and engaging in hobbies and activities that bring joy and relaxation. It is also important to make time for self-care and to prioritize it as a regular part of one's routine.

In conclusion, healing from narcissistic abuse is a journey that takes time and effort. It is important to be patient with oneself, to have self-compassion, and to prioritize self-care in order to create a healthy and fulfilling life. With the right support and resources, it is possible to heal from the trauma of narcissistic abuse and to create a life that is fulfilling and satisfying.

03: The Impact of Narcissistic Abuse on the Self-Esteem

The impact of narcissistic abuse on the self-esteem of the victim can be profound and long-lasting. Narcissistic abuse is characterized by a pattern of manipulation, control, and exploitation, and it can erode the victim's sense of self-worth and identity.

One of the defining characteristics of narcissistic abuse is that it is covert and insidious. Narcissists are often skilled at hiding their abusive behavior and may even present a charming and likable exterior to the world. This can make it difficult for victims of narcissistic abuse to recognize that they are being abused and to seek help.

The tactics that narcissists use in order to manipulate and control their victims can include gaslighting, triangulation, love bombing, isolation, economic abuse, emotional abuse, and physical abuse. These tactics can leave the victim feeling confused, isolated, and unsure of their own perceptions and feelings.

One of the most damaging aspects of narcissistic abuse is the way it can erode the victim's sense of self-worth and identity. Narcissists may use a range of tactics to chip away at their victim's self-esteem, including criticism, belittling, and manipulation. This can leave the victim feeling inadequate and unsure of their own value.

It is common for victims of narcissistic abuse to develop a sense of learned helplessness, in which they feel unable to make decisions or take action on their own. They may also develop a range of negative beliefs about themselves, such as believing that they are unworthy, defective, or unlovable. These negative beliefs can become deeply ingrained and can have a serious impact on the victim's self-esteem.

The impact of narcissistic abuse on the self-esteem of the victim can also extend to their relationships with others. Victims of narcissistic abuse may struggle to trust others and may have difficulty forming and maintaining healthy relationships. They may also have a difficult time setting boundaries and may struggle to assert themselves in healthy ways.

It is important to recognize that the impact of narcissistic abuse on the self-esteem of the victim can be long-lasting and can extend to other areas of their life. It can affect their mental health, their relationships, and their overall sense of well-being.

It is also important to recognize that the effects of narcissistic abuse can be healed and that it is possible to rebuild a healthy sense of self-worth and identity. Therapy can be a helpful resource in this process, as can connecting with others who have experienced similar abuse. It is also important to set boundaries, to learn to assert oneself in healthy ways, and to practice self-care in order to rebuild a healthy sense of self.

In conclusion, the impact of narcissistic abuse on the self-esteem of the victim can be profound and long-lasting. It can affect their mental health, their relationships, and their overall sense of well-being. However, it is possible to heal from the effects of narcissistic abuse and to rebuild a healthy sense of self-worth and identity with the right support and resources.

It is also important for individuals who have experienced narcissistic abuse to recognize that healing is a journey and that it is okay to take things one step at a time. It is important to be patient with oneself and to recognize that it is normal to have setbacks and difficult days.

It is also important to have self-compassion and to treat oneself with kindness and understanding. This can be especially difficult for individuals who have experienced narcissistic abuse, as their sense of self-worth may have been severely damaged. It is important to remind oneself that it is okay to make mistakes and that it is possible to learn from them and grow.

One way to practice self-compassion is through the use of affirmations. Affirmations are positive statements that can help to shift negative thought patterns and to rebuild a healthy sense of self-worth. Examples of affirmations that may be helpful for individuals who have experienced narcissistic abuse include:

– "I am worthy of love and respect."

– "I am deserving of healthy and fulfilling relationships."

– "I am capable of setting boundaries and taking care of myself."

– "I am enough just as I am."

03: THE IMPACT OF NARCISSISTIC ABUSE ON THE SELF-ESTEEM

It is also important to focus on self-care and to prioritize one's own well-being. This can include activities such as exercise, meditation, and engaging in hobbies and activities that bring joy and relaxation. It is also important to make time for self-care and to prioritize it as a regular part of one's routine.

In conclusion, healing from the impact of narcissistic abuse on the self-esteem is a journey that takes time and effort. It is important to be patient with oneself, to have self-compassion, and to prioritize self-care in order to rebuild a healthy sense of self-worth. With the right support and resources, it is possible to heal from the trauma of narcissistic abuse and to create a life that is fulfilling and satisfying.

It is also important for individuals who have experienced narcissistic abuse to recognize that they are not alone and that they are not to blame for the abuse they have suffered. It can be easy for victims of narcissistic abuse to internalize the blame and to believe that they are responsible for the abuse. It is important to recognize that the abuse is not the victim's fault and that they have the right to seek help and to create a healthy and fulfilling life for themselves.

It is also important to reach out for support. This can include talking to a therapist or counselor, reaching out to a support group, or contacting a domestic violence hotline for guidance and support. It can be helpful to connect with others who have experienced similar abuse, as it can provide a sense of understanding and community.

It is also important to remember that healing from narcissistic abuse takes time and that it is normal to have ups and downs in the process. It is important to be patient with oneself and to recognize that it is okay to take things one step at a time.

In conclusion, it is important for individuals who have experienced narcissistic abuse to recognize that they are not alone and that they are not to blame for the abuse they have suffered. It is important to seek support, to reach out for help, and to be patient with oneself in the healing process. With the right support and resources, it is possible to heal from the trauma of narcissistic abuse and to create a healthy and fulfilling life.

It is also important for individuals who have experienced narcissistic abuse to work on rebuilding their sense of self and their self-worth. This can be a difficult process, but it is an essential step in the healing journey. Therapy can be a helpful resource in this process, as can connecting with others who have experienced similar abuse.

One way to work on rebuilding a healthy sense of self is through the use of affirmations and positive self-talk. It can be helpful to write down affirmations and to repeat them to oneself on a daily basis. This can help to shift negative thought patterns and to rebuild a healthy sense of self-worth.

It can also be helpful to engage in activities that help to build self-esteem and to develop a sense of accomplishment. This can include setting and working towards goals, learning new skills, and participating in activities that bring joy and satisfaction.

It is also important to set boundaries and to learn to assert oneself in healthy ways. This can include learning how to say no, setting limits on what is acceptable behavior, and seeking support when needed. Setting boundaries is an important way to take care of oneself and to ensure that one's own needs and well-being are being met.

03: THE IMPACT OF NARCISSISTIC ABUSE ON THE SELF-ESTEEM

In conclusion, rebuilding a healthy sense of self and self-worth is an important part of the healing process after experiencing narcissistic abuse. It is important to engage in activities that help to build self-esteem, to set boundaries, and to practice self-care in order to rebuild a healthy sense of self. With the right support and resources, it is possible to heal from the trauma of narcissistic abuse and to create a life that is fulfilling and satisfying.

04: The Effects of Narcissistic Abuse on Emotional Health

The effects of narcissistic abuse on emotional health can be profound and long-lasting. Narcissistic abuse is characterized by a pattern of manipulation, control, and exploitation, and it can have serious consequences for the mental health of the victim.

One of the defining characteristics of narcissistic abuse is that it is covert and insidious. Narcissists are often skilled at hiding their abusive behavior and may even present a charming and likable exterior to the world. This can make it difficult for victims of narcissistic abuse to recognize that they are being abused and to seek help.

The tactics that narcissists use in order to manipulate and control their victims can include gaslighting, triangulation, love bombing, isolation, economic abuse, emotional abuse, and physical abuse. These tactics can leave the victim feeling confused, isolated, and unsure of their own perceptions and feelings.

One of the most damaging aspects of narcissistic abuse is the way it can affect the emotional health of the victim. It can lead to a range of mental health issues, including anxiety, depression, and post-traumatic stress disorder (PTSD).

Victims of narcissistic abuse may also struggle with emotional regulation and may have difficulty managing their emotions in a healthy way. They may have a tendency to suppress their emotions or to act out in unhealthy ways, such as lashing out at others or engaging in self-destructive behaviors.

It is important to recognize that the effects of narcissistic abuse on emotional health can be long-lasting and can extend to other areas of the victim's life. It can affect their relationships, their work, and their overall sense of well-being.

It is also important to recognize that the effects of narcissistic abuse on emotional health can be healed and that it is possible to rebuild a healthy emotional foundation. Therapy can be a helpful resource in this process, as can connecting with others who have experienced similar abuse. It is also important to practice self-care and to prioritize one's own well-being in order to rebuild emotional health.

04: THE EFFECTS OF NARCISSISTIC ABUSE ON EMOTIONAL HEALTH

In conclusion, the effects of narcissistic abuse on emotional health can be profound and long-lasting. It can lead to a range of mental health issues and can affect the victim's relationships, work, and overall sense of well-being. However, it is possible to heal from the effects of narcissistic abuse and to rebuild a healthy emotional foundation with the right support and resources.

It is also important for individuals who have experienced narcissistic abuse to seek support and to reach out for help. This can include talking to a therapist or counselor, reaching out to a support group, or contacting a domestic violence hotline for guidance and support. It can be helpful to connect with others who have experienced similar abuse, as it can provide a sense of understanding and community.

One way to work on rebuilding trust is through the use of affirmations and positive self-talk. It can be helpful to write down affirmations and to repeat them to oneself on a daily basis. This can help to shift negative thought patterns and to rebuild a healthy sense of trust in oneself.

It is also important to remember that healing from narcissistic abuse takes time and that it is normal to have ups and downs in the process. It is important to be patient with one-self and to recognize that it is okay to take things one step at a time.

It is also important to set boundaries and to learn to assert oneself in healthy ways. This can include learning how to say no, setting limits on what is acceptable behavior, and seeking support when needed. Setting boundaries is an important way to take care of oneself and to ensure that one's own needs and well-being are being met.

In conclusion, it is important for individuals who have experienced narcissistic abuse to seek support, to reach out for help, and to set boundaries in order to rebuild emotional health. It is important to be patient with oneself and to recognize that healing is a journey that takes time. With the right support and resources, it is possible to heal from the trauma of narcissistic abuse and to create a healthy and fulfilling life.

It is also important for individuals who have experienced narcissistic abuse to work on rebuilding their relationships with others. Narcissistic abuse can damage the victim's relationships with others and can make it difficult for them to trust and connect with others in a healthy way.

One way to work on rebuilding relationships is through the use of effective communication skills. This can include learning how to express one's needs and boundaries in a healthy way, listening actively to others, and being open and honest in communication.

It can also be helpful to engage in activities that help to build social connections and to develop a sense of community. This can include joining a support group, participating in hobbies and activities that bring joy and satisfaction, and volunteering in the community.

It is also important to set boundaries and to learn to assert oneself in healthy ways. This can include learning how to say no, setting limits on what is acceptable behavior, and seeking support when needed. Setting boundaries is an important way to take care of oneself and to ensure that one's own needs and well-being are being met.

In conclusion, rebuilding relationships with others is an important part of the healing process after experiencing narcissistic abuse. It is important to learn effective communication skills, to engage in activities that help to build social connections, and to set boundaries in order to rebuild healthy relationships. With the right support and resources, it is possible to heal from the trauma of narcissistic abuse and to create a healthy and fulfilling life.

05: The Dynamics of Narcissistic Relationships

The dynamics of narcissistic relationships are complex and can be difficult to understand. Narcissistic personality disorder is a mental health condition characterized by an inflated sense of self-importance, a need for admiration, and a lack of empathy for others. Narcissistic individuals may have a grandiose sense of self and may see themselves as superior to others.

In relationships, narcissists may use their charisma and charm to manipulate and control their partners. They may also engage in abusive behaviors, such as gaslighting, triangulation, love bombing, isolation, economic abuse, emotional abuse, and physical abuse. These tactics can leave the victim feeling confused, isolated, and unsure of their own perceptions and feelings.

One of the most challenging aspects of narcissistic relationships is the way that narcissists can change their behavior in order to manipulate their partners. They may be charming and loving at one moment and then turn cold and dismissive the next. This can make it difficult for the victim to trust their own perceptions and to understand what is happening in the relationship.

Narcissists may also engage in "love bombing," which is a tactic in which they shower their partners with affection and attention in the beginning stages of the relationship in order to win their trust and affection. This can be especially confusing for the victim, as it can make it difficult for them to see the narcissist's true intentions.

It is important to recognize that narcissistic relationships are not healthy and that they can have serious consequences for the victim's emotional and mental health. If you are in a narcissistic relationship, it is important to seek help and to get out of the relationship as soon as possible.

In conclusion, the dynamics of narcissistic relationships are complex and can be difficult to understand. Narcissistic individuals may use manipulation and abuse in order to control their partners and may engage in "love bombing" in the beginning stages of the relationship. It is important to recognize that narcissistic relationships are not healthy and to seek help if you are in one.

It is important to remember that leaving a narcissistic relationship can be challenging and that it may take time and effort. It is important to have a plan in place and to reach out for support from trusted friends, family, or a therapist.

It is also important to recognize that the victim of narciss- istic abuse is not to blame for the abuse they have suffered. Narcissistic individuals are responsible for their own beha- vior and for the harm they have caused.

It is also important to take care of oneself and to prioritize one's own well-being after leaving a narcissistic relation- ship. This can include seeking therapy, practicing self-care, and setting boundaries to ensure that one's own needs are being met.

It is also important to recognize that healing from narciss- istic abuse takes time and that it is normal to have ups and downs in the process. It is important to be patient with one- self and to recognize that it is okay to take things one step at a time.

In conclusion, leaving a narcissistic relationship can be challenging but it is an important step in the healing pro- cess. It is important to have a plan in place, to reach out for support, and to prioritize one's own well-being in order to rebuild a healthy and fulfilling life. It is also important to recognize that healing takes time and to be patient with oneself in the process.

It is important to remember that leaving a narcissistic relationship can be challenging and that it may take time and effort. It is important to have a plan in place and to reach out for support from trusted friends, family, or a therapist.

It is also important to recognize that the victim of narcissistic abuse is not to blame for the abuse they have suffered. Narcissistic individuals are responsible for their own behavior and for the harm they have caused.

It is also important to take care of oneself and to prioritize one's own well-being after leaving a narcissistic relationship. This can include seeking therapy, practicing self-care, and setting boundaries to ensure that one's own needs are being met.

It is also important to recognize that healing from narcissistic abuse takes time and that it is normal to have ups and downs in the process. It is important to be patient with oneself and to recognize that it is okay to take things one step at a time.

In conclusion, leaving a narcissistic relationship can be challenging but it is an important step in the healing process. It is important to have a plan in place, to reach out for support, and to prioritize one's own well-being in order to rebuild a healthy and fulfilling life. It is also important to recognize that healing takes time and to be patient with oneself in the process.

It is also important to recognize that healing from narcissistic abuse is a journey and that it is okay to take things one step at a time. It is important to be patient with oneself and to recognize that it is normal to have setbacks and difficult days.

It is also important to have self-compassion and to treat oneself with kindness and understanding. This can be especially difficult for individuals who have experienced narcissistic abuse, as their sense of self-worth may have been severely damaged. It is important to remind oneself that it is okay to make mistakes and that it is possible to learn from them and grow.

It is also important for individuals who have experienced narcissistic abuse to work on rebuilding their sense of trust and to learn to trust themselves again. Narcissistic abuse can shatter the victim's sense of trust in themselves and in others, and it can be difficult to rebuild this trust.

One way to work on rebuilding trust is through the use of affirmations and positive self-talk. It can be helpful to write down affirmations and to repeat them to oneself on a daily basis. This can help to shift negative thought patterns and to rebuild a healthy sense of trust in oneself.

It can also be helpful to engage in activities that help to build self-esteem and to develop a sense of accomplishment. This can include setting and working towards goals, learning new skills, and participating in activities that bring joy and satisfaction.

It is also important to set boundaries and to learn to assert oneself in healthy ways. This can include learning how to say no, setting limits on what is acceptable behavior, and seeking support when needed. Setting boundaries is an important way to take care of oneself and to ensure that one's own needs and well-being are being met.

In conclusion, rebuilding trust in oneself and in others is an important part of the healing process after experiencing narcissistic abuse. It is important to engage in activities that help to build self-esteem, to set boundaries, and to practice self-care in order to rebuild trust. With the right support and resources, it is possible to heal from the trauma of narcissistic abuse and to create a healthy and fulfilling life.

06: The Cycle of Narcissistic Abuse

The Cycle of Narcissistic Abuse is a term that describes the way in which narcissistic individuals and their relationships progress. It is not uncommon for victims of narcissistic abuse to feel confused and unsure of what is happening to them, and the cycle of abuse can be difficult to identify and understand. However, understanding this cycle can be an important step in breaking free from an abusive relationship and seeking help.

The cycle of narcissistic abuse begins with the "idealization" phase. In this phase, the narcissistic individual puts their partner on a pedestal, showering them with affection, attention, and flattery. They may promise their partner the world and make them feel special and loved. This phase can be intoxicating and can make the victim feel like they have found their perfect match.

However, the idealization phase is often short-lived, and it is eventually followed by the "devaluation" phase. In this phase, the narcissistic individual begins to tear down their partner and chip away at their self-esteem. They may criticize their partner's appearance, intelligence, or accomplishments, and they may belittle or dismiss their thoughts and feelings. They may also start to distance themselves emotionally, becoming cold and distant.

The victim of narcissistic abuse may try to please their partner and work to win back their love and affection during the devaluation phase. However, their efforts are often in vain, as the narcissistic individual is not capable of feeling genuine love or empathy.

The cycle of abuse is often followed by the "discard" phase, in which the narcissistic individual abruptly ends the relationship, leaving their partner heartbroken and confused. They may move on to a new partner and repeat the cycle, or they may simply move on without a replacement.

The victim of narcissistic abuse may feel a sense of relief upon the end of the relationship, but the emotional and psychological effects of the abuse can linger long after the relationship is over. They may struggle with feelings of worthlessness, self-doubt, and depression. They may also have difficulty trusting others and forming healthy relationships in the future.

It is important for victims of narcissistic abuse to seek help and support in order to heal and move on from the abuse. This may involve seeking therapy, joining a support group, or finding other resources to help them cope with the effects of the abuse.

It is also important for individuals to be aware of the signs of narcissistic abuse and to be cautious about entering into relationships with narcissistic individuals. Some warning signs of narcissistic abuse include a lack of empathy, a sense of entitlement, and an exaggerated sense of self-importance. It is also common for narcissistic individuals to manipulate and control their partners, and to use emotional abuse as a means of maintaining power and control in the relationship.

Breaking free from the cycle of narcissistic abuse can be a difficult and challenging process, but it is possible with the right support and resources. By seeking help and learning to recognize and avoid abusive relationships, individuals can take control of their lives and work towards a brighter, healthier future.

It is important to note that not all narcissistic individuals will follow the exact same cycle of abuse, and the length and intensity of each phase can vary. Some narcissistic individuals may remain in the idealization phase for longer periods of time, while others may move quickly through the cycle.

In some cases, the cycle of narcissistic abuse may involve "hoovering," in which the narcissistic individual tries to win back their partner after a period of abuse or abandonment. They may use tactics such as apologizing, promising to change, or showering their partner with attention and gifts in an attempt to regain their love and loyalty.

It is important for victims of narcissistic abuse to be aware of these tactics and to recognize that the narcissistic individual is not truly remorseful or committed to change. It is also important for victims to remember that they deserve love and respect, and to set boundaries and establish strict limits with their narcissistic partner.

Leaving a narcissistic relationship can be difficult, and it may involve facing intimidation, threats, and other forms of manipulation. It is important for victims to have a plan in place and to seek support from trusted friends, family members, or a domestic violence hotline.

Recovering from narcissistic abuse can be a long and difficult process, but it is possible with the right help and support. It is important for victims to take care of themselves and to prioritize their own well-being. This may involve seeking therapy, joining a support group, or finding other resources to help them cope with the effects of the abuse.

It is also important for individuals to educate themselves about narcissistic abuse and to be aware of the signs and dynamics of this type of abuse. By understanding the cycle of narcissistic abuse and learning to recognize and avoid abusive relationships, individuals can take control of their lives and work towards a brighter, healthier future.

In addition to seeking help and support, it is important for victims of narcissistic abuse to work on rebuilding their self-esteem and sense of worth. Narcissistic individuals often seek out and target individuals who are already struggling with self-doubt and low self-esteem, as they are more likely to be manipulated and controlled.

Victims of narcissistic abuse may benefit from activities and techniques that help to improve their self-esteem, such as positive affirmations, self-care practices, and setting and achieving personal goals. It can also be helpful to surround oneself with supportive and nurturing individuals who can provide love and encouragement.

It is also important for victims to recognize that the abuse they experienced was not their fault, and that they are not to blame for the behavior of their narcissistic partner. It can be helpful to work with a therapist or other mental health professional to process the abuse and to learn to let go of any feelings of responsibility or self-blame.

It can be challenging to move on and heal after experiencing narcissistic abuse, but it is possible with the right help and support. It is important for victims to remember that they are not alone, and that there are resources and support available to help them heal and rebuild their lives. With time, patience, and self-care, individuals can learn to let go of the past and move forward towards a brighter and healthier future.

In addition to seeking therapy and support from trusted individuals, there are a number of other steps that individuals can take to help them heal and recover from narcissistic abuse. Some additional tips for recovering from narcissistic abuse include:

– Practice self-care: It is important to prioritize self-care and to engage in activities that nourish and support your physical, emotional, and mental well-being. This may involve getting enough sleep, eating a healthy diet, exercising, and engaging in activities that bring joy and relaxation.

− Set boundaries: It is important to set clear boundaries with the narcissistic individual and to communicate your needs and limits to them. This may involve cutting off contact or limiting communication to specific times or places.

− Build a support system: Surrounding yourself with supportive and caring individuals can be a powerful tool in your recovery. Seek out friends and family members who can provide love, encouragement, and a listening ear. You may also consider joining a support group or connecting with other individuals who have experienced narcissistic abuse.

− Learn to recognize manipulation: Narcissistic individuals often use manipulation as a means of controlling and manipulating their partners. It is important to be aware of common manipulative tactics, such as gaslighting, love bombing, and triangulation, and to be prepared to stand up for yourself and set boundaries if these tactics are used against you.

– Seek professional help: Working with a therapist or other mental health professional can be a powerful tool in your recovery from narcissistic abuse. A therapist can help you process your experiences, work through your emotions, and develop coping strategies to deal with the aftermath of the abuse.

By following these tips and seeking help and support, individuals can take important steps towards healing and recovery from narcissistic abuse. With time and patience, it is possible to break free from the cycle of abuse and to build a brighter and healthier future.

It is important to note that recovery from narcissistic abuse is not a linear process, and it is common for individuals to experience setbacks and challenges along the way. It is normal to feel a range of emotions, including anger, sadness, fear, and confusion, and it is important to allow yourself the time and space to process these emotions.

It may also be helpful to remind yourself that the abuse was not your fault, and that you deserve love and respect. It can be helpful to work with a therapist or other mental health professional to help you work through any feelings of self-blame or guilt.

Another important aspect of recovery from narcissistic abuse is learning to establish healthy boundaries and to communicate effectively. Narcissistic individuals often rely on manipulation and control to maintain power in the relationship, and it is important to learn how to assert yourself and set clear limits with others.

It may also be helpful to practice self-compassion and to be kind and understanding towards yourself as you navigate the recovery process. It can be easy to fall into negative self-talk or to be overly critical of yourself, but it is important to remember that you are doing the best you can and that you deserve love and care.

Finally, it is important to remember that recovery is a journey, and that it may take time to heal and move on from the abuse. It is okay to take things one step at a time and to be patient with yourself as you work towards healing and recovery. With the right help and support, it is possible to break free from the cycle of narcissistic abuse and to build a brighter and healthier future.

07: The Trauma of Narcissistic Abuse

The trauma of narcissistic abuse can be deep and long-lasting, leaving victims feeling isolated, confused, and unsure of how to move forward. Narcissistic individuals often use manipulation, control, and emotional abuse as a means of maintaining power and control in the relationship, and the effects of this abuse can be devastating.

One of the most common forms of narcissistic abuse is gaslighting, which involves manipulating a victim into doubting their own perceptions and memories. The narcissistic individual may deny certain events or conversations took place, or they may twist the truth in order to make the victim feel confused and unsure of what is real. This can be extremely disorienting and can cause the victim to question their own sanity.

Another common form of narcissistic abuse is love bombing, in which the narcissistic individual showers their partner with excessive amounts of attention and affection in the beginning stages of the relationship. This can be intoxicating for the victim, who may feel like they have found their perfect match. However, this phase is often short-lived, and it is followed by a period of devaluation in which the narcissistic individual begins to tear down their partner and chip away at their self-esteem.

The trauma of narcissistic abuse can have a profound impact on a victim's emotional and psychological well-being. They may struggle with feelings of worthlessness, self-doubt, and depression. They may also have difficulty trusting others and forming healthy relationships in the future.

The effects of narcissistic abuse can also extend to a victim's physical health. Stress and anxiety, common responses to abuse, can have a range of physical symptoms, including insomnia, headaches, and stomach problems. The constant emotional rollercoaster of an abusive relationship can also take a toll on the immune system, making individuals more susceptible to illness.

It is important for victims of narcissistic abuse to seek help and support in order to heal and move on from the trauma. This may involve seeking therapy, joining a support group, or finding other resources to help them cope with the effects of the abuse. It is also important for victims to practice self-care and to prioritize their own well-being as they work towards recovery.

It is important to recognize that recovery from narcissistic abuse is a process and that it may take time to heal and move on from the trauma. It is normal to experience setbacks and challenges along the way, and it is important to be patient with oneself and to allow oneself the time and space to process and heal.

By seeking help and support, practicing self-care, and setting boundaries, victims of narcissistic abuse can take important steps towards healing and recovery. With time and patience, it is possible to break free from the cycle of abuse and to build a brighter, healthier future.

It is important for victims of narcissistic abuse to understand that the trauma they have experienced is real and that it is not their fault. Narcissistic individuals are often skilled at manipulating and controlling their partners, and they may use tactics such as gaslighting and love bombing to confuse and disorient their victims.

It can be helpful for victims to educate themselves about narcissistic abuse and to learn about the common tactics that narcissistic individuals use. This can help them to recognize when they are being manipulated or controlled, and to take steps to protect themselves and set boundaries.

It is also important for victims of narcissistic abuse to seek support and validation from trusted friends, family members, or a therapist. It can be easy to feel isolated and alone after experiencing abuse, and having a supportive network of people can be crucial in the recovery process.

Another important aspect of recovery from the trauma of narcissistic abuse is learning to practice self-compassion and to be kind and understanding towards oneself. It is common for victims of abuse to struggle with feelings of self-blame and to be overly critical of themselves. It is important to remember that the abuse was not your fault, and that you deserve love and care.

Finally, it is important to remember that recovery from narcissistic abuse is a journey, and that it may take time to heal and move on from the trauma. It is okay to take things one step at a time and to be patient with yourself as you work towards healing and recovery. With the right help and support, it is possible to break free from the cycle of abuse and to build a brighter and healthier future.

It is important for victims of narcissistic abuse to understand that they are not alone, and that there are resources and support available to help them heal and recover from the trauma. Some additional resources that may be helpful for victims of narcissistic abuse include:

– Domestic violence hotlines: Many domestic violence hotlines offer support, resources, and counseling for individuals who have experienced abuse. These hotlines can be a safe and confidential way to get help and to find out about additional resources in your area.

– Support groups: Joining a support group can be a helpful way to connect with other individuals who have experienced narcissistic abuse. Support groups can provide a sense of community, as well as a place to share experiences and receive support and guidance.

– Therapy: Working with a therapist or other mental health professional can be a powerful tool in your recovery from narcissistic abuse. A therapist can help you process your experiences, work through your emotions, and develop coping strategies to deal with the aftermath of the abuse.

– Online resources: There are many online resources available for individuals who have experienced narcissistic abuse. These resources can provide information, support, and guidance for those who are seeking to heal and recover from the trauma.

By seeking out these resources and seeking help and support, individuals can take important steps towards healing and recovery from narcissistic abuse. With time and patience, it is possible to break free from the cycle of abuse and to build a brighter and healthier future.

It is important for victims of narcissistic abuse to understand that recovery is a process, and that it may take time to heal and move on from the trauma. It is normal to experience setbacks and challenges along the way, and it is important to be patient with oneself and to allow oneself the time and space to process and heal.

It can be helpful for victims of narcissistic abuse to develop a self-care routine that includes activities that nourish and support their physical, emotional, and mental well-being. This may involve getting enough sleep, eating a healthy diet, exercising, and engaging in activities that bring joy and relaxation.

It is also important for victims to set boundaries and to communicate their needs and limits to others. This may involve cutting off contact or limiting communication with the narcissistic individual or setting limits with other people in your life.

Another important aspect of recovery is building a support system of trusted friends, family members, or a therapist. It can be helpful to have people who can provide love, encouragement, and a listening ear as you work through the recovery process.

Finally, it is important to remember that recovery is a journey, and that it may take time to heal and move on from the trauma. It is okay to take things one step at a time and to be patient with yourself as you work towards healing and recovery. With the right help and support, it is possible to break free from the cycle of abuse and to build a brighter and healthier future.

08: Healing from Narcissistic Abuse

Healing from narcissistic abuse can be a difficult and complex process. Narcissistic abuse is a form of emotional abuse that is inflicted upon a person by a narcissistic individual, who is characterized by an inflated sense of self-importance and a lack of empathy.

The first step in healing from narcissistic abuse is to acknowledge that you have been a victim of abuse. This can be difficult to do, as narcissistic individuals are often skilled at manipulating and controlling their victims, leading them to doubt their own perceptions and experiences. It is important to remember that abuse is never the victim's fault, and that it is not uncommon for victims to have been subjected to gaslighting, which is a form of manipulation that causes the victim to doubt their own memories and perceptions.

Once you have acknowledged that you have been a victim of narcissistic abuse, it is important to seek support from friends, family, or a professional therapist. It can be helpful to speak with someone who can provide an outside perspective and validate your experiences.

It is also important to set boundaries and establish firm limits with the narcissistic individual in your life. This can be challenging, as narcissistic individuals often do not respect boundaries and may attempt to manipulate or control you in order to get their way. However, setting boundaries is crucial in protecting yourself from further abuse and in reclaiming your power.

It is also essential to practice self-care and prioritize your own well-being. This can involve activities such as exercising, getting enough rest, eating a healthy diet, and engaging in activities that bring you joy and relaxation. It is also important to find ways to manage your stress and cope with the trauma of the abuse. This may involve seeking out support from a therapist or counselor, joining a support group, or finding healthy ways to cope with your emotions such as through journaling or practicing mindfulness.

Another important aspect of healing from narcissistic abuse is learning to love and accept yourself. Narcissistic abuse can erode a victim's sense of self-worth and leave them feeling unworthy of love and affection. It is important to remind yourself that you are deserving of love and respect, and to work on building self-confidence and self-esteem.

This can involve engaging in activities that allow you to express yourself creatively, setting and achieving personal goals, and learning to appreciate your own unique qualities and strengths.

It can also be helpful to educate yourself about narcissistic abuse and the tactics that narcissistic individuals use to manipulate and control their victims. This can help you to recognize and defend against these tactics, and to understand the motivations behind the abuse.

Ultimately, healing from narcissistic abuse is a journey that requires patience, self-compassion, and a strong support network. It is important to take things one day at a time and to be gentle with yourself as you work through the healing process. With time, support, and self-care, it is possible to overcome the effects of narcissistic abuse and to rebuild a sense of self-worth and empowerment.

It is also important to work on rebuilding healthy relationships with others. Narcissistic abuse can leave victims feeling isolated and disconnected from others, and it is common for victims to have difficulty trusting others after experiencing abuse. It is important to seek out supportive and healthy relationships, and to work on rebuilding trust with others. This may involve seeking out therapy or joining a support group to work on these issues.

It is also important to work on developing healthy communication skills and learning how to assert your needs and boundaries. This may involve setting limits with others, saying no when appropriate, and learning how to effectively communicate your thoughts and feelings. It can also be helpful to learn how to set and respect boundaries with others, and to recognize when a boundary has been crossed.

Another important aspect of healing from narcissistic abuse is learning to forgive both yourself and the narcissistic individual. Forgiveness does not mean condoning the abuse or absolving the abuser of responsibility, but rather it involves releasing feelings of anger, resentment, and bitterness. Forgiveness can be a difficult process, and it may involve seeking support from a therapist or counselor.

It is also important to remember that healing is a journey and not a destination. It is normal to have ups and downs and to experience setbacks along the way. It is important to be patient with yourself and to recognize that healing takes time.

In conclusion, healing from narcissistic abuse is a complex and difficult process that requires patience, self-compassion, and support. It involves acknowledging the abuse, seeking support, setting boundaries, practicing self-care, rebuilding self-worth, and learning to forgive. With time, support, and self-care, it is possible to overcome the effects of narcissistic abuse and to rebuild a sense of self-worth and empowerment.

It is also important to recognize that healing from narcissistic abuse can be a long-term process, and it may take time to fully understand the impact that the abuse has had on your life. It is important to be patient with yourself and to recognize that it is normal to have good days and bad days as you work through the healing process.

It can be helpful to engage in activities that promote healing and self-care, such as exercising, practicing mindfulness, or engaging in hobbies or activities that bring you joy and relaxation. It is also important to surround yourself with supportive and understanding people who can provide a listening ear and offer encouragement and validation.

It can be helpful to seek out therapy or counseling to work through the emotional and psychological effects of the abuse. A therapist or counselor can provide a safe and supportive space to process your thoughts and feelings and to work on building healthy coping mechanisms.

It is also important to remember that healing from narcissistic abuse is not about returning to the relationship with the narcissistic individual. Instead, it is about moving forward and rebuilding your life in a healthy and empowering way. This may involve finding ways to disconnect from the narcissist, whether through setting boundaries or severing contact altogether.

In summary, healing from narcissistic abuse is a complex and long-term process that requires patience, self-compassion, and support. It involves acknowledging the abuse, seeking support, setting boundaries, practicing self-care, rebuilding self-worth, and learning to forgive. With time, support, and self-care, it is possible to overcome the effects of narcissistic abuse and to rebuild your life in a healthy and empowering way.

It is also important to recognize that healing from narcissistic abuse is not a linear process and that there may be set-backs along the way. It is common to experience a range of emotions as you work through the healing process, and it is important to allow yourself to feel and process these emotions in a healthy way.

It can be helpful to develop healthy coping mechanisms to manage the stress and emotions that may arise as you work through the healing process. This may involve practicing mindfulness, finding healthy outlets for stress such as exercise or creative expression, or seeking support from a therapist or counselor.

It is also important to practice self-compassion and to be kind to yourself as you navigate the healing process. This may involve setting aside time for self-care, such as taking a warm bath or going for a walk, or engaging in activities that bring you joy and relaxation.

It is also important to remember that healing from narciss-istic abuse is not about forgetting the abuse or minimizing its impact. It is about acknowledging the abuse, processing the emotions that it has caused, and finding healthy ways to cope with and move beyond the abuse.

In conclusion, healing from narcissistic abuse is a complex and long-term process that requires patience, self-compassion, and support. It involves acknowledging the abuse, seeking support, setting boundaries, practicing self-care, rebuilding self-worth, and learning to forgive. With time, support, and self-care, it is possible to overcome the effects of narcissistic abuse and to rebuild your life in a healthy and empowering way. Remember to be patient with yourself, to practice self-compassion, and to seek out support as you work through the healing process.

09: Coping Strategies for Surviving Narcissistic Abuse

Surviving narcissistic abuse can be a challenging and overwhelming experience, and it is important to have coping strategies in place to help you get through it. Narcissistic abuse is a form of emotional abuse that is inflicted upon a person by a narcissistic individual, who is characterized by an inflated sense of self-importance and a lack of empathy.

One important coping strategy for surviving narcissistic abuse is to establish and maintain strong boundaries. Boundaries are limits that you set with others to protect yourself and to establish what is and is not acceptable behavior. It is important to set boundaries with the narcissistic individual in your life, as they may attempt to manipulate or control you in order to get their way. Setting boundaries can be challenging, as narcissistic individuals often do not respect boundaries, but it is crucial in protecting yourself from further abuse and in reclaiming your power.

Another coping strategy is to seek out a support network of trusted friends, family, or a professional therapist. It can be helpful to speak with someone who can provide an outside perspective and validate your experiences. It is also important to find healthy outlets for your emotions, such as through journaling, talking to a trusted friend or family member, or seeking support from a therapist or counselor.

It is also important to practice self-care and prioritize your own well-being. This can involve activities such as exercising, getting enough rest, eating a healthy diet, and engaging in activities that bring you joy and relaxation. It is also important to find ways to manage your stress and cope with the trauma of the abuse. This may involve seeking out support from a therapist or counselor, joining a support group, or finding healthy ways to cope with your emotions such as through mindfulness or other stress-reduction techniques.

It is also essential to educate yourself about narcissistic abuse and the tactics that narcissistic individuals use to manipulate and control their victims. This can help you to recognize and defend against these tactics, and to understand the motivations behind the abuse. This can be especially helpful in situations where you may still be in contact with the narcissistic individual, as it can give you the knowledge and tools you need to protect yourself from further abuse.

Another coping strategy is to find ways to disconnect from

the narcissistic individual and to create a sense of distance between yourself and the abuse. This may involve setting limits with the narcissistic individual, such as limiting contact or establishing boundaries, or it may involve severing contact altogether. It is important to remember that you have the right to make decisions about your own well-being and to create space for yourself if that is what you need.

It is also important to work on rebuilding your self-worth and self-esteem, as narcissistic abuse can erode these qualities. This may involve engaging in activities that allow you to express yourself creatively, setting and achieving personal goals, and learning to appreciate your own unique qualities and strengths. It can also be helpful to seek out therapy or counseling to work on building self-worth and self-esteem.

Ultimately, coping with narcissistic abuse is a journey that requires patience, self-compassion, and a strong support network. It is important to take things one day at a time and to be gentle with yourself as you work through the healing process. With time, support, and self-care, it is possible to survive narcissistic abuse and to rebuild a sense of self-worth and empowerment.

Another coping strategy is to find healthy ways to cope with the emotions that may arise as a result of the abuse. It is common for victims of narcissistic abuse to experience a range of emotions, including anger, sadness, fear, and guilt. It is important to allow yourself to feel and process these emotions in a healthy way, rather than bottling them up or trying to suppress them.

One way to cope with these emotions is through self-expression, such as through journaling, art, or music. It can also be helpful to engage in activities that allow you to express your emotions in a healthy way, such as through exercise or creative pursuits.

It is also important to seek out healthy outlets for your emotions, such as through talking to a trusted friend or family member, seeking support from a therapist or counselor, or joining a support group. These outlets can provide a safe space to process your thoughts and feelings and can help you to feel less alone as you navigate the challenges of surviving narcissistic abuse.

Another coping strategy is to focus on the present moment and to take things one day at a time. It can be overwhelming to think about the long-term impacts of the abuse, and it is important to focus on what you can control in the present moment. This may involve setting small, achievable goals for yourself, such as going for a walk or spending time with a supportive friend.

It is also important to practice self-compassion and to be kind to yourself as you navigate the challenges of surviving narcissistic abuse. This may involve setting aside time for self-care, such as taking a warm bath or going for a walk, or engaging in activities that bring you joy and relaxation. It is also important to remember that it is okay to have bad days and to give yourself permission to feel and process your emotions.

In conclusion, coping with narcissistic abuse is a challenging and complex process that requires patience, self-compassion, and support. It involves establishing and maintaining boundaries, seeking support, practicing self-care, finding healthy outlets for emotions, educating yourself about narcissistic abuse, and focusing on the present moment.

09: COPING STRATEGIES FOR SURVIVING NARCISS-ISTIC ABUSE

With time, support, and self-care, it is possible to survive narcissistic abuse and to rebuild a sense of self-worth and empowerment. Remember to be patient with yourself, to practice self-compassion, and to seek out support as you navigate the challenges of surviving narcissistic abuse.

Another coping strategy is to find healthy ways to cope with the aftermath of the abuse, including the trauma and the feelings of grief and loss that may arise. It is common for victims of narcissistic abuse to experience feelings of grief and loss, as they may have lost a sense of self, a sense of trust, or important relationships as a result of the abuse.

One way to cope with these feelings is through therapy or counseling, which can provide a safe and supportive space to process your thoughts and feelings and to work through the grief and loss. It can also be helpful to join a support group, where you can connect with others who have experienced similar challenges and who can provide a sense of community and support.

Another coping strategy is to find healthy outlets for your emotions, such as through talking to a trusted friend or family member, writing in a journal, or engaging in activities that bring you joy and relaxation. It is also important to practice self-care and to prioritize your own well-being, as this can help you to manage the stress and emotions that may arise as you work through the aftermath of the abuse.

It is also important to practice forgiveness, both for yourself and for the narcissistic individual. Forgiveness does not mean condoning the abuse or absolving the abuser of responsibility, but rather it involves releasing feelings of anger, resentment, and bitterness. Forgiveness can be a difficult process, and it may involve seeking support from a therapist or counselor.

It is also important to remember that healing from narcissistic abuse is a journey and not a destination. It is normal to have ups and downs and to experience setbacks along the way. It is important to be patient with yourself and to recognize that healing takes time.

In conclusion, coping with the aftermath of narcissistic abuse is a complex and challenging process that requires patience, self-compassion, and support. It involves finding healthy outlets for emotions, seeking therapy or counseling, practicing self-care, practicing forgiveness, and being patient with yourself. With time, support, and self-care, it is possible to work through the aftermath of narcissistic abuse and to rebuild a sense of self-worth and empowerment. Remember to be patient with yourself, to practice self-compassion, and to seek out support as you work through the challenges of surviving narcissistic abuse.

10: The Role of Therapy in Healing from Narcissistic Abuse

The role of therapy in healing from narcissistic abuse is significant and can be instrumental in helping individuals to work through the emotional and psychological effects of the abuse. Narcissistic abuse is a form of emotional abuse that is inflicted upon a person by a narcissistic individual, who is characterized by an inflated sense of self-importance and a lack of empathy.

One important role of therapy is to provide a safe and supportive space for individuals to process their thoughts and feelings about the abuse. Therapy can provide a place to express and explore the emotions that may arise as a result of the abuse, including anger, sadness, fear, and guilt. It can also provide a space to work through the trauma of the abuse and to develop healthy coping mechanisms.

Another role of therapy is to help individuals to develop healthy coping skills and to build resilience in the face of the challenges that may arise as a result of the abuse. This may involve teaching individuals how to manage their stress and emotions, how to set and maintain boundaries, and how to practice self-care.

10: THE ROLE OF THERAPY IN HEALING FROM NARCISSISTIC ABUSE

Therapy can also play a role in helping individuals to rebuild their self-worth and self-esteem, which may have been eroded as a result of the abuse. This may involve working on building self-confidence and self-acceptance, and learning to appreciate and value one's own unique qualities and strengths.

In addition, therapy can be helpful in helping individuals to develop healthy communication skills and to assert their needs and boundaries. This may involve learning how to effectively express thoughts and feelings, how to set limits with others, and how to recognize when a boundary has been crossed.

Another role of therapy is to help individuals to work through the process of forgiveness, both for themselves and for the narcissistic individual. Forgiveness does not mean condoning the abuse or absolving the abuser of responsibility, but rather it involves releasing feelings of anger, resentment, and bitterness. Forgiveness can be a difficult process, and therapy can provide a safe and supportive space to work through these emotions.

Finally, therapy can help individuals to develop a sense of

empowerment and to rebuild their lives in a healthy and positive way. This may involve working on goals and aspirations, finding ways to disconnect from the narcissistic individual, and building healthy relationships with others.

In conclusion, therapy plays a crucial role in healing from narcissistic abuse. It provides a safe and supportive space to process thoughts and feelings, to develop healthy coping skills and resilience, to rebuild self-worth and self-esteem, to develop healthy communication skills and assertiveness, to work through the process of forgiveness, and to rebuild one's life in a healthy and empowering way. If you are a victim of narcissistic abuse, consider seeking out the support of a qualified therapist or counselor to help you on your journey towards healing and recovery.

Another role of therapy in healing from narcissistic abuse is to help individuals to recognize the patterns of abuse and to understand the tactics that narcissistic individuals use to manipulate and control their victims. This can be especially important in situations where the individual may still be in contact with the narcissistic individual, as it can help them to recognize and defend against these tactics, and to understand the motivations behind the abuse.

Therapy can also be helpful in helping individuals to heal from the trauma of the abuse, which may involve working through the grief and loss that may arise as a result of the abuse. This may involve exploring the impact of the abuse on the individual's sense of self, their relationships, and their sense of trust.

Another role of therapy is to help individuals to develop healthy relationship skills and to rebuild healthy relationships with others. Narcissistic abuse can leave victims feeling isolated and disconnected from others, and it is common for victims to have difficulty trusting others after experiencing abuse. Therapy can provide a safe space to work on rebuilding trust and to learn how to establish and maintain healthy relationships.

It is also important to recognize that healing from narcissistic abuse is a journey and not a destination. It is normal to have ups and downs and to experience setbacks along the way. Therapy can help individuals to be patient with themselves and to recognize that healing takes time.

10: THE ROLE OF THERAPY IN HEALING FROM NARCISSISTIC ABUSE

In conclusion, therapy plays a crucial role in healing from narcissistic abuse. It provides a safe and supportive space to process thoughts and feelings, to develop healthy coping skills and resilience, to rebuild self-worth and self-esteem, to develop healthy communication skills and assertiveness, to work through the process of forgiveness, and to rebuild one's life in a healthy and empowering way. It can also help individuals to recognize patterns of abuse, to heal from the trauma of the abuse, and to rebuild healthy relationships with others. If you are a victim of narcissistic abuse, consider seeking out the support of a qualified therapist or counselor to help you on your journey towards healing and recovery.

Narcissistic abuse can be a deeply traumatic and devastating experience for those who have gone through it. It can leave individuals feeling confused, hurt, and unsure of how to move forward with their lives. Therapy can be an essential part of the healing process for those who have experienced narcissistic abuse, as it provides a safe and supportive environment in which to process and make sense of the abuse.

10: THE ROLE OF THERAPY IN HEALING FROM NARCISSISTIC ABUSE

The first step in healing from narcissistic abuse is often acknowledging that the abuse has occurred and that it was not the victim's fault. It can be difficult for individuals who have experienced narcissistic abuse to confront the reality of the abuse, as they may have been made to feel as though they were at fault or that they were responsible for the abuser's behavior. However, it is important to recognize that the abuser is solely responsible for their own actions and that the victim is not to blame for the abuse.

Once an individual has acknowledged the abuse and accepted that it was not their fault, the next step is often to work on rebuilding a sense of self-worth and self-esteem. Narcissistic abusers often seek to undermine their victims' confidence and self-worth, leaving them feeling unsure of themselves and their own value. Therapy can be helpful in this process, as it allows individuals to explore their own thoughts and feelings and to work on rebuilding a positive sense of self.

It is also common for individuals who have experienced narcissistic abuse to struggle with feelings of anxiety, depression, and post-traumatic stress disorder (PTSD). Therapy can be an important tool in addressing and managing these feelings, helping individuals to develop coping mechanisms and to learn how to regulate their emotions.

In addition to individual therapy, group therapy can also be beneficial for those who have experienced narcissistic abuse. Group therapy provides a sense of community and support, allowing individuals to connect with others who have experienced similar situations and to share their experiences and insights. Group therapy can also be helpful in normalizing the feelings and experiences of those who have been through narcissistic abuse, as it allows individuals to see that they are not alone and that others have been through similar experiences.

It is important for individuals who are seeking therapy for narcissistic abuse to find a therapist who is experienced in working with this type of abuse. A therapist who is knowledgeable about narcissistic abuse can provide valuable support and guidance as individuals work through the healing process. It is also important for individuals to feel comfortable and safe with their therapist, as this will facilitate a more productive and beneficial therapeutic relationship.

10: THE ROLE OF THERAPY IN HEALING FROM NAR-CISSISTIC ABUSE

In conclusion, therapy can play a crucial role in healing from narcissistic abuse. By providing a safe and supportive environment in which to process the abuse and rebuild a sense of self-worth, therapy can help individuals to move forward with their lives and to reclaim their sense of agency and autonomy. If you or someone you know has experienced narcissistic abuse, seeking out therapy can be an important step in the healing process.

11: The Importance of Self-Care after Narcissistic Abuse

Self-care is an essential part of the healing process after experiencing narcissistic abuse. Narcissistic abuse can be a deeply traumatic and devastating experience, leaving individuals feeling drained, exhausted, and unsure of how to move forward. It is important for individuals to prioritize their own well-being and to take care of themselves in order to facilitate healing and recovery.

One of the first steps in the self-care process is to prioritize self-compassion. It is common for individuals who have experienced narcissistic abuse to blame themselves for the abuse, feeling as though they could have done something to prevent it. It is important to remember that the abuse was not the victim's fault and that they are not to blame for the abuser's behavior. Practicing self-compassion can help individuals to let go of self-blame and to be kind and understanding towards themselves as they heal.

Another important aspect of self-care is taking time for oneself. After experiencing narcissistic abuse, it is common for individuals to feel overwhelmed and burnt out. It is important to take time for oneself and to prioritize one's own needs and desires. This can include activities such as getting enough rest, engaging in hobbies and activities that bring joy, and setting boundaries with others.

It is also important to practice good self-care habits, such as maintaining a healthy diet, getting regular exercise, and engaging in relaxation techniques such as meditation or yoga. These habits can help to reduce stress and promote overall well-being.

In addition to physical self-care, it is also important to prioritize emotional and mental well-being. This can include seeking out therapy to process the abuse and to work through any lingering emotions or trauma. It can also be helpful to practice mindfulness and to engage in activities that promote emotional well-being, such as journaling or talking to a trusted friend or family member.

It is important to remember that self-care looks different for everyone and that what works for one person may not work for another. It is important to experiment and find what works best for oneself in terms of self-care.

It is also important to recognize that self-care is not selfish.

11: THE IMPORTANCE OF SELF-CARE AFTER NARCISS-ISTIC ABUSE

Taking care of oneself is necessary in order to be able to effectively care for others and to fully engage in one's life. It is not a luxury, but rather a necessity for healing and recovery.

In conclusion, self-care is an essential part of the healing process after experiencing narcissistic abuse. By prioritizing self-compassion, taking time for oneself, and practicing good self-care habits, individuals can facilitate their own healing and recovery and work towards rebuilding their lives.

It can be challenging to prioritize self-care after experiencing narcissistic abuse, especially if the abuser was controlling or manipulative. It may be necessary to set boundaries with the abuser and to limit or cut off contact in order to prioritize one's own well-being. This can be difficult, especially if there are shared children or financial ties, but it is important to prioritize one's own safety and well-being.

It can also be helpful to seek out a support system of trusted friends and family members who can provide emotional support and practical assistance as needed. It is important to surround oneself with people who are supportive and understanding and who can provide a sense of community as one navigates the healing process.

It is also important to recognize that healing from narcissistic abuse is a journey and that it may not happen overnight. It is normal to have ups and downs and to experience a range of emotions as one processes the abuse and works towards healing. It is important to be patient with oneself and to allow oneself the time and space to heal at one's own pace.

In conclusion, the importance of self-care after experiencing narcissistic abuse cannot be overstated. By prioritizing self-compassion, taking time for oneself, and seeking out a supportive network of friends and family, individuals can begin to rebuild their lives and to move forward in a positive and healthy way. It is a journey, but with patience and self-care, healing is possible.

It is also important to recognize that healing from narcissistic abuse is not a linear process and that there may be setbacks along the way. It is common for individuals to experience triggers that can bring up memories of the abuse and to feel overwhelmed by emotions. It is important to have coping mechanisms in place to deal with these triggers and to take care of oneself during these times.

It may be necessary to seek additional support during times of increased stress or difficulty. This can include seeking out therapy or support groups, or even taking a break from certain activities or responsibilities to focus on self-care. It is important to prioritize one's own well-being and to do what is necessary to take care of oneself during these times.

It is also important to remember that healing from narcissistic abuse is not about forgetting the past or pretending that the abuse never happened. It is about acknowledging the abuse and the impact it had, and then finding ways to move forward and to create a healthy and fulfilling life. This may involve setting boundaries, learning to advocate for oneself, and finding ways to cope with the lasting effects of the abuse.

It is also important to recognize that healing is not a solo journey and that it is okay to ask for help. It can be difficult to navigate the healing process on one's own, and seeking out support and guidance from trusted friends, family, or a therapist can be an important part of the process.

11: THE IMPORTANCE OF SELF-CARE AFTER NARCISS-ISTIC ABUSE

In conclusion, healing from narcissistic abuse is a complex and nuanced process that requires patience, self-compassion, and a willingness to prioritize one's own well-being. It is a journey that involves acknowledging the past and the impact of the abuse, while also finding ways to move forward and create a healthy and fulfilling life. By seeking out support and practicing self-care, individuals can work towards healing and towards creating a life that is meaningful and fulfilling.

Another aspect of healing from narcissistic abuse is learning to recognize and avoid toxic or abusive relationships in the future. This may involve learning to set boundaries, assert oneself, and advocate for one's own needs and desires. It can also involve learning to recognize the warning signs of narcissistic abuse, such as a lack of empathy, a tendency towards manipulation or control, and a focus on one's own needs at the expense of others.

It can be helpful to work with a therapist or coach who is experienced in working with individuals who have experienced narcissistic abuse, as they can provide guidance and support as one navigates the process of recognizing and avoiding toxic relationships. It may also be helpful to seek out resources and support groups that can provide additional guidance and support.

In addition to seeking out support and learning to recognize and avoid toxic relationships, it is also important to focus on self-growth and personal development. This can involve finding activities and hobbies that bring joy and meaning, setting goals and working towards achieving them, and finding ways to express oneself and one's unique talents and interests.

Self-growth and personal development can be an important part of the healing process, as it allows individuals to move beyond the trauma of the abuse and to create a life that is fulfilling and meaningful. It can also help to rebuild a sense of self-worth and confidence, which may have been damaged as a result of the abuse.

In conclusion, healing from narcissistic abuse involves a range of activities and strategies, including seeking out support, practicing self-care, learning to recognize and avoid toxic relationships, and focusing on self-growth and personal development. By engaging in these activities, individuals can work towards rebuilding their lives and towards creating a future that is healthy, fulfilling, and free from abuse.

12: Breaking the Cycle: How to Avoid Narcissistic Relationships

Narcissistic relationships can be deeply damaging and traumatic, leaving individuals feeling hurt, confused, and unsure of how to move forward. It is important for individuals who have experienced narcissistic abuse to take steps to break the cycle and to avoid future narcissistic relationships.

One of the first steps in breaking the cycle is to educate oneself about narcissistic personality disorder and the signs of narcissistic abuse. It is important to recognize the patterns of behavior that are typical of narcissistic individuals and to be aware of the warning signs of narcissistic abuse. Some common signs of narcissistic abuse include a lack of empathy, a tendency towards manipulation or control, and a focus on one's own needs at the expense of others.

It is also important to recognize the ways in which narcissistic individuals may try to manipulate or control their victims. Narcissistic individuals may try to gaslight their victims, making them doubt their own perceptions and memories. They may also try to isolate their victims from friends and family, making them feel dependent on the abuser. By being aware of these tactics, individuals can better protect themselves from falling victim to narcissistic abuse.

In addition to educating oneself about narcissistic personality disorder and the signs of narcissistic abuse, it is also important to set boundaries and to assert oneself in relationships. This may involve setting limits on what one is willing to tolerate in a relationship and standing up for oneself when those boundaries are violated. It may also involve learning to advocate for one's own needs and desires and to communicate openly and honestly with others.

It can be helpful to seek out support and guidance from trusted friends and family members, as well as from therapists or coaches who are experienced in working with individuals who have experienced narcissistic abuse. These individuals can provide valuable perspective and guidance as one navigates the process of breaking the cycle and avoiding future narcissistic relationships.

It is also important to prioritize self-care and to focus on one's own well-being. This may involve setting aside time for oneself, engaging in activities that bring joy and meaning, and practicing good self-care habits such as maintaining a healthy diet and getting regular exercise. Taking care of oneself can help to build confidence and self-worth, which can be important in avoiding future narcissistic relationships.

In conclusion, breaking the cycle of narcissistic relationships involves educating oneself about narcissistic personality disorder and the signs of narcissistic abuse, setting boundaries and asserting oneself, seeking out support, and prioritizing self-care. By engaging in these activities, individuals can better protect themselves from falling victim to narcissistic abuse and can work towards creating healthy, fulfilling relationships in the future.

It is also important to recognize that breaking the cycle of narcissistic relationships is a process and that it may not happen overnight. It may take time to unlearn patterns of behavior that have been reinforced by past narcissistic relationships and to develop new, healthier ways of relating to others. It is important to be patient with oneself and to allow oneself the time and space to work through this process.

It may also be helpful to work on building self-esteem and self-worth. Narcissistic individuals often seek out individuals with low self-esteem, as they are more likely to be swayed by the abuser's manipulations. By building a strong sense of self-worth and self-esteem, individuals can become more resilient to the manipulations of narcissistic individuals.

It is also important to recognize that it is not uncommon for individuals who have experienced narcissistic abuse to attract narcissistic individuals in the future. This may be due to a pattern of seeking out individuals who will reinforce negative beliefs about oneself, or it may be a result of a lack of awareness of the warning signs of narcissistic abuse. It is important to be aware of this pattern and to actively work to break it by educating oneself about narcissistic personality disorder and the signs of narcissistic abuse, setting boundaries, and seeking out supportive and healthy relationships.

In conclusion, breaking the cycle of narcissistic relationships involves a range of activities and strategies, including educating oneself about narcissistic personality disorder, setting boundaries and asserting oneself, seeking out support, prioritizing self-care, and working on building self-esteem and self-worth. By engaging in these activities, individuals can better protect themselves from falling victim to narcissistic abuse and can work towards creating healthy, fulfilling relationships in the future. It is a process, but with patience and persistence, it is possible to break the cycle and to create a life that is free from narcissistic abuse.

It is also important to recognize that breaking the cycle of narcissistic relationships is not just about avoiding narciss- istic individuals, but also about healing from the trauma of the abuse. This may involve seeking out therapy to process the abuse and to work through any lingering emotions or trauma. It may also involve finding ways to cope with the lasting effects of the abuse, such as anxiety, depression, or post-traumatic stress disorder (PTSD).

It is important to recognize that healing from narcissistic abuse is a journey and that it may take time. It is normal to have ups and downs and to experience a range of emotions as one processes the abuse and works towards healing. It is important to be patient with oneself and to allow oneself the time and space to heal at one's own pace.

In addition to seeking out therapy, it can be helpful to find other sources of support, such as support groups or trusted friends and family members. It is important to surround oneself with individuals who are supportive and understanding and who can provide a sense of community as one navigates the healing process.

It is also important to recognize that breaking the cycle of narcissistic relationships is not about forgetting the past or pretending that the abuse never happened. It is about acknowledging the abuse and the impact it had, and then finding ways to move forward and to create a healthy and fulfilling life. This may involve setting boundaries, learning to advocate for oneself, and finding ways to cope with the lasting effects of the abuse.

In conclusion, breaking the cycle of narcissistic relationships involves not just avoiding narcissistic individuals, but also healing from the trauma of the abuse. This may involve seeking out therapy, finding support, and focusing on self-care and self-growth. By engaging in these activities, individuals can work towards healing and towards creating a future that is healthy, fulfilling, and free from abuse.

It may also be helpful to work on building healthy communication skills as a way to break the cycle of narcissistic relationships. Narcissistic individuals often use communication as a way to manipulate and control their victims, and learning healthy communication skills can help individuals to protect themselves from falling victim to this type of abuse.

Healthy communication skills include the ability to express oneself clearly and assertively, to listen actively and empathetically, and to resolve conflicts in a healthy way. It may be helpful to seek out resources or training on healthy communication skills or to work with a therapist or coach who can provide guidance and support in this area.

Another important aspect of breaking the cycle of narcissistic relationships is learning to recognize and trust one's own instincts and boundaries. It is common for individuals who have experienced narcissistic abuse to doubt their own perceptions and to feel unsure of what they want and need. It is important to tune in to one's own feelings and to listen to one's own needs and desires. Setting boundaries and advocating for oneself can be an important part of this process.

It is also important to recognize that breaking the cycle of narcissistic relationships does not mean that all relationships will be perfect or free from conflict. Healthy relationships involve give and take and require effort and communication from both parties. However, by learning to recognize and trust one's own instincts and boundaries and by building healthy communication skills, individuals can work towards creating relationships that are healthy, fulfilling, and free from abuse.

In conclusion, breaking the cycle of narcissistic relationships involves a range of activities and strategies, including seeking out therapy, finding support, practicing self-care and self-growth, building healthy communication skills, and learning to recognize and trust one's own instincts and boundaries. By engaging in these activities, individuals can work towards healing from the trauma of narcissistic abuse and towards creating a future that is healthy, fulfilling, and free from abuse.

13: Moving Forward: Building a Healthy Life after Narcissistic Abuse

Moving forward and building a healthy life after experiencing narcissistic abuse can be a challenging but rewarding process. It involves acknowledging the abuse and the impact it had, while also finding ways to move beyond the trauma and to create a fulfilling and meaningful life.

One of the first steps in this process is to prioritize self-care and to take care of one's own well-being. This may involve setting aside time for oneself, engaging in activities that bring joy and meaning, and practicing good self-care habits such as maintaining a healthy diet and getting regular exercise. It is important to remember that self-care is not selfish, but rather a necessary part of the healing process and of building a healthy life.

Another important aspect of moving forward is seeking out support and guidance from trusted friends and family members, as well as from therapists or coaches who are experienced in working with individuals who have experienced narcissistic abuse. These individuals can provide valuable perspective and guidance as one navigates the process of healing and building a healthy life.

It is also important to work on building healthy communication skills and to learn how to effectively advocate for oneself and one's own needs and desires. This may involve setting boundaries and learning to assert oneself in relationships. It may also involve learning to recognize and avoid toxic or abusive relationships in the future.

In addition to these strategies, it can be helpful to focus on self-growth and personal development. This may involve finding activities and hobbies that bring joy and meaning, setting goals and working towards achieving them, and finding ways to express oneself and one's unique talents and interests. Self-growth and personal development can be an important part of the healing process, as it allows individuals to move beyond the trauma of the abuse and to create a life that is fulfilling and meaningful.

It is also important to recognize that moving forward and building a healthy life after narcissistic abuse is a journey and that it may not happen overnight. It is normal to have ups and downs and to experience a range of emotions as one processes the abuse and works towards healing. It is important to be patient with oneself and to allow oneself the time and space to heal at one's own pace.

In conclusion, moving forward and building a healthy life after narcissistic abuse involves a range of activities and strategies, including prioritizing self-care, seeking out support, building healthy communication skills, focusing on self-growth and personal development, and being patient with oneself. By engaging in these activities, individuals can work towards healing from the trauma of narcissistic abuse and towards creating a future that is healthy, fulfilling, and free from abuse.

It can also be helpful to find ways to cope with the lasting effects of the abuse, such as anxiety, depression, or post-traumatic stress disorder (PTSD). This may involve seeking out therapy or support groups, or finding healthy ways to manage stress, such as through exercise or relaxation techniques.

It is important to recognize that healing from narcissistic abuse is a process and that it may involve revisiting and processing difficult emotions and memories. It is normal to experience a range of emotions as one works through the healing process, and it is important to allow oneself the time and space to process these emotions in a healthy way.

It may also be helpful to find ways to connect with others who have experienced similar types of abuse. Support groups or online communities can provide a sense of community and a sense of connection with others who understand the unique challenges and experiences of narcissistic abuse.

Another important aspect of moving forward and building a healthy life is learning to forgive oneself for any perceived mistakes or for staying in the abusive relationship for longer than one wished. It is important to recognize that narcissistic abuse is often characterized by manipulation and control, and that it is not the victim's fault. It is also important to recognize that healing is a process and that it is normal to have setbacks along the way.

In conclusion, moving forward and building a healthy life after narcissistic abuse involves a range of activities and strategies, including seeking out therapy or support, finding healthy ways to cope with the lasting effects of the abuse, connecting with others who have experienced similar types of abuse, and learning to forgive oneself. By engaging in these activities, individuals can work towards healing from the trauma of narcissistic abuse and towards creating a future that is healthy, fulfilling, and free from abuse.

It can also be helpful to work on rebuilding one's sense of self and one's sense of identity after experiencing narcissistic abuse. Narcissistic individuals often attempt to manipulate and control their victims by undermining their sense of self and their sense of identity. Rebuilding a strong sense of self and a healthy sense of identity can be an important part of the healing process.

This may involve finding activities and hobbies that bring joy and meaning, setting goals and working towards achieving them, and finding ways to express oneself and one's unique talents and interests. It may also involve seeking out therapy or support to work through any lingering issues related to self-esteem or self-worth.

It is also important to recognize that moving forward and building a healthy life after narcissistic abuse is not about forgetting the past or pretending that the abuse never happened. It is about acknowledging the abuse and the impact it had, and then finding ways to move forward and to create a healthy and fulfilling life. This may involve setting boundaries, learning to advocate for oneself, and finding ways to cope with the lasting effects of the abuse.

In conclusion, moving forward and building a healthy life after narcissistic abuse involves a range of activities and strategies, including seeking out therapy or support, finding healthy ways to cope with the lasting effects of the abuse, connecting with others who have experienced similar types of abuse, learning to forgive oneself, and rebuilding a strong sense of self and identity. It is a journey that requires patience, self-compassion, and a willingness to prioritize one's own well-being. By engaging in these activities and strategies, individuals can work towards healing from the trauma of narcissistic abuse and towards creating a future that is healthy, fulfilling, and free from abuse.

It is also important to recognize that moving forward does not mean that all challenges or difficulties will disappear. Life is unpredictable and there will always be ups and downs. However, by focusing on self-care, seeking out support, and building healthy coping skills, individuals can work towards building a strong foundation of resilience that will help them to navigate life's challenges and to create a healthy, fulfilling life.

It is also important to remember that it is okay to ask for help when needed. It is not uncommon for individuals who have experienced narcissistic abuse to feel isolated or unsupported, and seeking out help and support from trusted friends, family, or a therapist can be an important part of the healing process.

In conclusion, moving forward and building a healthy life after narcissistic abuse involves a range of activities and strategies, including prioritizing self-care, seeking out support, building healthy coping skills, rebuilding a strong sense of self and identity, and remembering that it is okay to ask for help when needed. By engaging in these activities, individuals can work towards healing from the trauma of narcissistic abuse and towards creating a future that is healthy, fulfilling, and free from abuse. It is important to recognize that this process takes time and requires patience, self-compassion, and a willingness to prioritize one's own well-being.

One final aspect of moving forward and building a healthy life after narcissistic abuse is finding ways to let go of the past and to create a new future. This may involve finding ways to forgive the abuser, either for oneself or as a way to move on from the abuse. It may also involve finding ways to let go of the pain and trauma of the abuse and to focus on building a new, healthy life.

This process may involve finding ways to cope with any lingering feelings of anger, hurt, or resentment. It may also involve finding healthy ways to express and process these emotions, such as through therapy or journaling. It is important to recognize that letting go of the past is a process and that it may take time, but it is an important step in moving forward and building a healthy life after narcissistic abuse.

In conclusion, moving forward and building a healthy life after narcissistic abuse involves a range of activities and strategies, including prioritizing self-care, seeking out support, building healthy coping skills, rebuilding a strong sense of self and identity, remembering that it is okay to ask

for help when needed, and finding ways to let go of the past
and to create a new future. By engaging in these activities,
individuals can work towards healing from the trauma of
narcissistic abuse and towards creating a future that is
healthy, fulfilling, and free from abuse.

Book 3 - Co-dependency

A Practical and Empowering Guide to Recognizing and Overcoming the Patterns of Codependency in Your Life: From the Roots of Childhood Trauma to the Steps of Healing and Self-Discovery

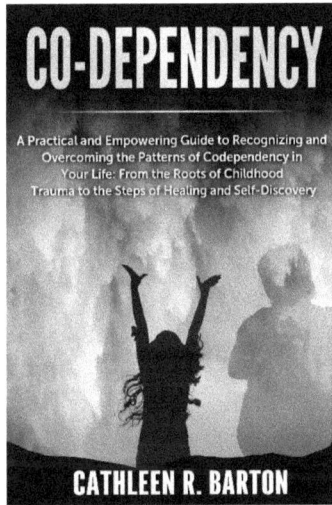

01: What is Co-dependency?

Co-dependency is a term used to describe a type of unhealthy and dysfunctional behavior that can occur in relationships. It is characterized by an excessive emotional, physical, and psychological reliance on another person, often to the point where an individual's own needs and desires are neglected or suppressed.

At its core, co-dependency is a pattern of relating to others that is characterized by a lack of healthy boundaries and an inability to be autonomous. It is often rooted in childhood trauma or the experience of growing up in an unhealthy or dysfunctional family system.

There are many different ways that co-dependency can manifest in relationships. Some common characteristics of co-dependent behavior include:

– Putting the needs of others before your own

– Seeking validation and approval from others

– Struggling to make decisions for yourself

– Feeling responsible for the feelings and actions of others

01: WHAT IS CO-DEPENDENCY?

– Difficulty saying "no" or setting boundaries

– Difficulty identifying and expressing your own emotions

– Difficulty with self-care and self-worth

Co-dependency can be harmful to both the individual exhibiting the behavior and the people they are in relationships with. It can lead to feelings of resentment, low self-esteem, and a lack of fulfillment in life. It can also contribute to the development of unhealthy patterns of communication and interaction in relationships.

Co-dependency is often associated with unhealthy relationships, such as those that are marked by codependent behavior, abuse, or neglect. However, it is important to note that co-dependency can also occur in seemingly healthy and functional relationships.

If you think you may be in a co-dependent relationship, it is important to seek help. There are many resources available to support you in recognizing and overcoming co-dependent behavior, including therapy, support groups, and self-help books and materials.

01: WHAT IS CO-DEPENDENCY?

Breaking the cycle of co-dependency can be a challenging process, but it is also an empowering and rewarding journey. By learning to set healthy boundaries, communicate effectively, and prioritize your own needs and desires, you can create more fulfilling and healthy relationships with yourself and others.

There are a few key steps that can be helpful in overcoming co-dependency and building healthier relationships:

– Identify your co-dependent behaviors: The first step in overcoming co-dependency is to become aware of the patterns of behavior that contribute to it. This may involve seeking the help of a therapist or joining a support group, where you can gain insight into your own behavior and how it affects your relationships.

– Set healthy boundaries: Setting healthy boundaries is an important aspect of overcoming co-dependency. This means learning to say "no" when you feel overwhelmed or taken advantage of, and establishing clear limits and expectations in your relationships.

– Practice self-care: Co-dependency can often be fueled by a lack of self-care and self-worth. By taking care of your own needs and developing a strong sense of self, you can become more autonomous and less reliant on others for validation and fulfillment.

– Seek support: Overcoming co-dependency can be a difficult process, and it is often helpful to have the support of others. This can include seeking the help of a therapist or joining a support group where you can connect with others who are also working on overcoming co-dependent behavior.

– Learn healthy communication skills: Developing healthy communication skills can be an important aspect of overcoming co-dependency. This includes learning how to express your own needs and boundaries, as well as how to listen to and respect the needs and boundaries of others.

By taking these steps, you can begin to break the cycle of co-dependency and build healthier, more fulfilling relationships with yourself and others. Remember, overcoming co-dependency is a journey, and it may take time and effort. Be patient with yourself, and remember that seeking help and support is an important aspect of the process.

It is important to note that overcoming co-dependency is a

process that may take time and effort. It is not uncommon for individuals to experience setbacks or relapses along the way. If this happens, it is important to be kind to yourself and remember that recovery is a journey, not a destination.

If you feel like you are struggling to overcome co-dependency, it may be helpful to seek the help of a therapist or coach who can provide guidance and support. Therapy can be a safe and supportive space to explore your feelings, thoughts, and behaviors, and to develop new strategies for coping and healing.

In addition to seeking professional help, there are also several self-care strategies that you can try to help you on your journey of recovery. These may include:

– Engaging in activities that bring you joy and relaxation, such as hobbies, exercise, or spending time in nature

– Practicing mindfulness and other stress-reducing techniques, such as deep breathing, meditation, or yoga

– Seeking support from friends and loved ones who are supportive and non-judgmental

01: WHAT IS CO-DEPENDENCY?

– Seeking out healthy role models or mentors who can provide guidance and inspiration

By incorporating these self-care strategies into your daily routine, you can build resilience, reduce stress, and create a sense of balance in your life.

Ultimately, the key to overcoming co-dependency is to prioritize your own needs and well-being. By learning to take care of yourself, set healthy boundaries, and communicate effectively, you can build stronger, more fulfilling relationships with yourself and others.

It is also important to be mindful of the potential for co-dependent behavior to resurface in the future. This is especially true if you have a history of co-dependency in your relationships or if you are returning to a previous relationship where co-dependent patterns were present.

To reduce the risk of relapse, it can be helpful to:

– Stay connected to a support network, such as a therapy group or a support group for individuals recovering from co-dependency

– Continue to practice self-care and prioritize your own needs and well-being

– Communicate openly and honestly with your partner or loved ones about your needs and boundaries

– Seek additional support if you feel overwhelmed or like you are losing ground in your recovery

By being mindful of the potential for co-dependent behavior to resurface and taking proactive steps to prevent it, you can increase your chances of long-term recovery and build healthier, more fulfilling relationships.

Remember, overcoming co-dependency is a journey that requires patience, self-compassion, and a commitment to personal growth. With time, effort, and the right support, you can break the cycle of co-dependency and create more fulfilling, healthy relationships with yourself and others.

02: The Roots of Co-dependency: Understanding Childhood Trauma

Co-dependency is often rooted in early life experiences, particularly those that occur during childhood. Many individuals who struggle with co-dependent behavior have a history of childhood trauma or grew up in unhealthy or dysfunctional family systems.

Childhood trauma can take many forms, including physical, sexual, or emotional abuse; neglect; household dysfunction; or exposure to other traumatic events. These experiences can have a profound and lasting impact on an individual's development and sense of self, and can lay the foundation for co-dependent patterns of behavior later in life.

One way in which childhood trauma can lead to co-dependency is through the development of unhealthy coping mechanisms. When faced with difficult or overwhelming experiences, children may learn to suppress their emotions or to put the needs of others before their own in order to feel a sense of control or to avoid further harm. These coping strategies may provide some short-term relief, but they can

189

also become ingrained patterns of behavior that continue into adulthood, leading to co-dependent relationships.

Another way in which childhood trauma can contribute to co-dependency is through the development of a negative self-image. Children who have experienced trauma may internalize negative messages about themselves, leading to low self-esteem and a lack of self-worth. This can make it difficult for individuals to assert their own needs and boundaries, leading to co-dependent patterns of behavior.

It is important to note that not everyone who has experienced childhood trauma will go on to struggle with co-dependency. However, it is common for individuals with a history of trauma to be more vulnerable to co-dependent patterns of behavior, and it is important to be aware of this connection.

If you think that your co-dependent behavior may be rooted in childhood trauma, it is important to seek help. Therapy can be a valuable resource for individuals who want to explore their past experiences and work through the challenges that they have faced. With the help of a trained therapist, you can learn to cope with your past in healthy ways and build a more fulfilling and autonomous life.

It is also important to be patient with yourself and to re-member that healing from childhood trauma is a journey, not a destination. It may take time to work through the challenges that you have faced and to develop new, health-ier patterns of behavior. With time, effort, and the right support, you can overcome the roots of co-dependency and build a more fulfilling and self-sufficient life.

There are a few key steps that you can take to begin healing from the roots of co-dependency and childhood trauma:

– Seek therapy: Working with a trained therapist can be a valuable resource for individuals who want to explore the impact of their past experiences on their present lives. Ther-apy can provide a safe and supportive space to process and work through difficult emotions, and to develop new coping strategies and patterns of behavior.

– Practice self-care: Taking care of yourself is an important aspect of healing from childhood trauma. This may involve engaging in activities that bring you joy and relaxation, such as hobbies, exercise, or spending time in nature. It may also involve practicing self-compassion and learning to treat yourself with kindness and understanding.

– Seek support: It can be helpful to have the support of others as you work through the challenges of healing from childhood trauma. This may include seeking the help of a therapist or joining a support group, or simply spending time with friends and loved ones who are supportive and non-judgmental.

– Explore your feelings and thoughts: It can be helpful to spend time exploring your feelings and thoughts about your past experiences. This may involve writing in a journal, talking with a therapist or trusted friend, or participating in activities that allow you to express yourself creatively.

– Learn healthy coping strategies: Developing healthy coping strategies can be an important aspect of healing from childhood trauma. This may include learning how to manage stress and regulate your emotions, or practicing mindfulness and other stress-reducing techniques, such as deep breathing, meditation, or yoga.

By taking these steps, you can begin to heal from the roots

of co-dependency and childhood trauma and build a more fulfilling and autonomous life. Remember, healing is a journey, and it may take time and effort. Be patient with yourself, and remember that seeking help and support is an important aspect of the process.

It is important to recognize that healing from childhood trauma and overcoming co-dependent patterns of behavior is a process that may involve ups and downs. There may be times when you feel like you are making progress, and other times when you feel stuck or overwhelmed. This is a normal part of the process, and it is important to be kind to yourself and to remember that healing takes time.

If you feel like you are struggling to overcome co-dependency or to heal from childhood trauma, it may be helpful to seek additional support. This may involve seeking the help of a therapist or coach, joining a support group, or connecting with others who are also working on overcoming similar challenges.

It can also be helpful to have a plan in place for managing setbacks or difficult emotions. This may involve identifying healthy coping strategies, such as talking with a trusted friend, engaging in self-care activities, or practicing mind-fulness, that you can turn to when you are feeling over-whelmed or triggered.

By being proactive and seeking support when needed, you can increase your chances of success in overcoming co-dependency and healing from childhood trauma. Remember, you are not alone, and there are many resources available to help you on your journey of recovery.

In addition to seeking professional help and support, there are also a few self-care strategies that you can try to help you on your journey of healing from childhood trauma and overcoming co-dependency. These may include:

– Engaging in activities that bring you joy and relaxation: Taking time to do things that you enjoy can be an important aspect of self-care and can help you to manage stress and cope with difficult emotions. This may include hobbies, ex-ercise, spending time in nature, or any other activity that brings you a sense of pleasure and relaxation.

– Practicing mindfulness and other stress-reducing tech-niques: Techniques such as deep breathing, meditation, or

yoga can be helpful in reducing stress and promoting relaxation. By taking time to focus on the present moment and
your breath, you can cultivate a sense of calm and clarity
that can help you to cope with challenging emotions.

– Seeking support from friends and loved ones: It can be
helpful to have the support of others as you work through
the challenges of healing from childhood trauma and overcoming co-dependency. Surrounding yourself with supportive and non-judgmental people can provide a sense of connection and belonging, and can help you to feel less alone.

– Seeking out healthy role models or mentors: Having
someone to look up to or to provide guidance and inspiration can be an important aspect of healing and personal
growth. Consider seeking out a mentor or role model who
has overcome similar challenges and can offer guidance and
support as you work to build a more fulfilling life.

By incorporating these self-care strategies into your daily
routine, you can build resilience, reduce stress, and create a
sense of balance in your life. Remember, healing from childhood trauma and overcoming co-dependency is a journey
that requires patience, self-compassion, and a commitment

to personal growth. With time, effort, and the right support, you can create a more fulfilling and healthy life for yourself.

03: Recognizing Co-dependent Behaviors in Yourself and Others

One of the first steps in overcoming co-dependency is to become aware of the patterns of behavior that contribute to it. This can be challenging, as co-dependent behavior is often deeply ingrained and may be difficult to recognize. However, by being mindful of the signs and symptoms of co-dependency, you can begin to identify co-dependent behaviors in yourself and others and take steps to address them.

Some common signs of co-dependent behavior include:

– Putting the needs of others before your own

– Seeking validation and approval from others

– Struggling to make decisions for yourself

– Feeling responsible for the feelings and actions of others

– Difficulty saying "no" or setting boundaries

– Difficulty identifying and expressing your own emotions

– Difficulty with self-care and self-worth

03: RECOGNIZING CO-DEPENDENT BEHAVIORS IN YOURSELF AND OTHERS

If you recognize any of these behaviors in yourself or in someone you are close to, it may be worth exploring the possibility of co-dependency.

It is important to note that co-dependent behavior is often learned through experience, particularly in the context of unhealthy or dysfunctional relationships. If you have a history of co-dependent relationships or grew up in a family system that was marked by co-dependent patterns of behavior, you may be more vulnerable to co-dependency.

If you think that you or someone you know may be struggling with co-dependency, it is important to seek help. There are many resources available to support you in recognizing and overcoming co-dependent behavior, including therapy, support groups, and self-help books and materials.

By becoming more aware of co-dependent behaviors in yourself and others, you can take the first step towards building healthier, more fulfilling relationships. Remember, overcoming co-dependency is a journey, and it may take time and effort. Be patient with yourself, and remember that seeking help and support is an important aspect of the process.

03: RECOGNIZING CO-DEPENDENT BEHAVIORS IN YOURSELF AND OTHERS

There are a few key steps that you can take to begin recognizing and addressing co-dependent behaviors in yourself and others:

– Seek therapy: Working with a trained therapist can be a valuable resource for individuals who want to explore co-dependent patterns of behavior and learn new ways of relating to others. Therapy can provide a safe and supportive space to process and work through difficult emotions, and to develop new coping strategies and patterns of behavior.

– Join a support group: Support groups can be a helpful resource for individuals who are working to overcome co-dependency. These groups provide a space to connect with others who are also struggling with similar challenges, and to learn from each other's experiences and insights.

– Read self-help books and materials: There are many self-help books and materials available that can provide guidance and support for individuals who are working to overcome co-dependent behavior. Reading about the experiences of others and learning about effective strategies for change can be a valuable resource on your journey of recovery.

03: RECOGNIZING CO-DEPENDENT BEHAVIORS IN YOURSELF AND OTHERS

– Practice self-care: Taking care of yourself is an important aspect of overcoming co-dependency. This may involve engaging in activities that bring you joy and relaxation, such as hobbies, exercise, or spending time in nature. It may also involve practicing self-compassion and learning to treat yourself with kindness and understanding.

By taking these steps, you can begin to recognize and address co-dependent behaviors in yourself and others, and build healthier, more fulfilling relationships. Remember, overcoming co-dependency is a journey that requires patience, self-compassion,and a commitment to personal growth. It may take time and effort to identify and address co-dependent behaviors, and there may be setbacks along the way. However, by seeking help and support, practicing self-care, and being patient with yourself, you can increase your chances of success in overcoming co-dependency and building healthier relationships.

It is also important to remember that overcoming co-dependency is not just about changing your own behavior, but also about learning to interact with others in a more healthy and autonomous way. This may involve setting and respecting boundaries, learning how to communicate effectively, and building self-worth and self-confidence.

By taking these steps, you can begin to build healthier, more fulfilling relationships with yourself and others, and create a more fulfilling and self-sufficient life. Remember, you are not alone, and there are many resources available to help you on your journey of recovery. With time, effort, and the right support, you can overcome co-dependency and create a more fulfilling and healthy life for yourself.

Another important aspect of overcoming co-dependency is learning how to set and maintain healthy boundaries. Boundaries are the limits we set in our relationships with others that help us to feel safe and respected. They can be physical, emotional, or mental, and they help us to communicate our needs and desires, and to protect ourselves from being taken advantage of or mistreated.

Setting and maintaining healthy boundaries can be challenging, especially if you have a history of co-dependency or have grown up in a family system that did not model healthy boundaries. However, learning to set and respect boundaries is an important aspect of building healthy, autonomous relationships.

Here are a few tips for setting and maintaining healthy boundaries:

– Identify your needs and values: The first step in setting boundaries is to know what you need and what is important to you. Take time to reflect on your own feelings, needs, and values, and be clear about what you are and are not willing to accept in your relationships.

– Communicate your boundaries: Once you have identified your needs and values, it is important to communicate them to others. This may involve saying "no" when you are not comfortable with a request, or expressing your needs and desires in a clear and direct way.

– Respect the boundaries of others: Just as it is important to communicate your own boundaries, it is also important to respect the boundaries of others. This means listening to and acknowledging the needs and desires of others, and being willing to compromise and negotiate when necessary.

– Practice self-care: Taking care of yourself is an important aspect of setting and maintaining healthy boundaries. This may involve setting aside time for yourself, engaging in activities that bring you joy and relaxation, or seeking the help of a therapist or coach if you are struggling to set and maintain boundaries.

By following these tips, you can learn to set and maintain healthy boundaries in your relationships, and build healthier, more fulfilling connections with yourself and others. Remember, setting and respecting boundaries is an ongoing process, and it may take time and effort to develop healthy habits. Be patient with yourself, and seek help if you need it. With time, effort, and the right support, you can learn to set and maintain healthy boundaries and build stronger, more autonomous relationships.

04: The Costs of Co-dependency: How it Affects Your Relationships and Mental Health

Co-dependency can have a profound impact on an individual's relationships and mental health. It can lead to a range of negative consequences, including:

– Difficulty building and maintaining healthy relationships: Co-dependent behavior can make it difficult for individuals to build and maintain healthy, fulfilling relationships. This may be due to a lack of healthy communication and boundaries, or a tendency to put the needs of others before one's own. As a result, co-dependency can lead to feelings of loneliness, isolation, and frustration.

– Difficulty with self-care and self-worth: Co-dependent behavior can also make it difficult for individuals to take care of themselves and to prioritize their own needs. This can lead to a lack of self-worth and self-esteem, and to feelings of inadequacy and worthlessness.

– Mental health challenges: Co-dependency can also have a negative impact on an individual's mental health. It can lead to increased stress and anxiety, as well as to symptoms

of depression. It can also make it more difficult for individuals to cope with challenging emotions and situations,
leading to a greater risk of mental health problems.

– Interpersonal conflict: Co-dependent behavior can also
contribute to interpersonal conflict and strained relationships. This may be due to a lack of healthy communication
and boundary-setting, or to a tendency to put the needs of
others before one's own. This can lead to feelings of resentment and anger, and to a lack of trust and emotional intimacy in relationships.

Overall, co-dependency can have a range of negative consequences that can affect an individual's relationships and
mental health. It is important to be aware of these potential
costs and to take steps to address co-dependent behavior in
order to build healthier, more fulfilling relationships and
improve overall well-being.

If you are struggling with co-dependency and want to overcome its negative effects on your relationships and mental
health, there are a few key steps that you can take:

– Seek therapy: Working with a trained therapist can be a

valuable resource for individuals who want to explore co-dependent patterns of behavior and learn new ways of relating to others. Therapy can provide a safe and supportive space to process and work through difficult emotions, and to develop new coping strategies and patterns of behavior.

– Join a support group: Support groups can be a helpful resource for individuals who are working to overcome co-dependency. These groups provide a space to connect with others who are also struggling with similar challenges, and to learn from each other's experiences and insights.

– Read self-help books and materials: There are many self-help books and materials available that can provide guidance and support for individuals who are working to overcome co-dependent behavior. Reading about the experiences of others and learning about effective strategies for change can be a valuable resource on your journey of recovery.

– Practice self-care: Taking care of yourself is an important aspect of overcoming co-dependency. This may involve engaging in activities that bring you joy and relaxation, such as hobbies, exercise, or spending time in nature. It may also involve practicing self-compassion and learning to treat yourself with kindness and understanding.

By taking these steps, you can begin to address co-dependent patterns of behavior and build healthier, more fulfilling relationships. Remember, overcoming co-dependency is a journey that requires patience, self-compassion, and a commitment to personal growth. It may take time and effort to identify and address co-dependent behaviors, and there may be setbacks along the way. However, by seeking help and support, practicing self-care, and being patient with yourself, you can increase your chances of success in overcoming co-dependency and building healthier relationships.

In addition to seeking professional help and support, there are also a few self-care strategies that you can try to help you on your journey of overcoming co-dependency and improving your relationships and mental health. These may include:

– Engaging in activities that bring you joy and relaxation: Taking time to do things that you enjoy can be an important aspect of self-care and can help you to manage stress and cope with difficult emotions. This may include hobbies, exercise, spending time in nature, or any other activity that brings you a sense of pleasure and relaxation.

– Practicing mindfulness and other stress-reducing techniques: Techniques such as deep breathing, meditation, or yoga can be helpful in reducing stress and promoting relaxation. By taking time to focus on the present moment and your breath, you can cultivate a sense of calm and clarity that can help you to cope with challenging emotions.

– Seeking support from friends and loved ones: It can be helpful to have the support of others as you work to overcome co-dependency and improve your relationships and mental health. Surrounding yourself with supportive and non-judgmental people can provide a sense of connection and belonging, and can help you to feel less alone.

– Seeking out healthy role models or mentors: Having someone to look up to or to provide guidance and inspiration can be an important aspect of personal growth and healing. Consider seeking out a mentor or role model who has overcome similar challenges and can offer guidance and support as you work to build a more fulfilling life.

By incorporating these self-care strategies into your daily routine, you can build resilience, reduce stress, and create a sense of balance in your life. Remember, overcomingco-dependency and improving your relationships and mental health is a journey that requires patience, self-compassion, and a commitment to personal growth. With time, effort, and the right support, you can create a more fulfilling and healthy life for yourself.

It is also important to remember that healing and personal growth is an ongoing process, and it is normal to have ups and downs along the way. If you find that you are struggling to make progress or are feeling overwhelmed, it may be helpful to seek additional support. This may involve talking with a therapist or coach, joining a support group, or connecting with others who are also working on overcoming similar challenges.

By being proactive and seeking help when needed, you can increase your chances of success in overcoming co-dependency and improving your relationships and mental health. Remember, you are not alone, and there are many resources available to help you on your journey of recovery. With the right support and a commitment to personal growth, you can build a more fulfilling and healthy life for yourself.

05: Breaking the Cycle of Co-dependency: Setting Boundaries and Finding Empowerment

Breaking the cycle of co-dependency and finding empowerment can be a challenging but ultimately rewarding process. It involves learning how to set and maintain healthy boundaries, developing a sense of self-worth and self-sufficiency, and building healthier, more fulfilling relationships. While it may take time and effort, the benefits of breaking the cycle of co-dependency are numerous, including increased well-being, improved mental health, and stronger, more fulfilling relationships.

One of the key steps in breaking the cycle of co-dependency is learning how to set and maintain healthy boundaries. Boundaries are the limits we set in our relationships with others that help us to feel safe and respected. They can be physical, emotional, or mental, and they help us to communicate our needs and desires, and to protect ourselves from being taken advantage of or mistreated.

Setting and maintaining healthy boundaries can be challenging, especially if you have a history of co-dependency or have grown up in a family system that did not model healthy boundaries. However, learning to set and respect boundaries is an important aspect of building healthy, autonomous relationships.

Here are a few tips for setting and maintaining healthy boundaries:

– Identify your needs and values: The first step in setting boundaries is to know what you need and what is important to you. Take time to reflect on your own feelings, needs, and values, and be clear about what you are and are not willing to accept in your relationships.

– Communicate your boundaries: Once you have identified your needs and values, it is important to communicate them to others. This may involve saying "no" when you are not comfortable with a request, or expressing your needs and desires in a clear and direct way.

– Respect the boundaries of others: Just as it is important to communicate your own boundaries, it is also important to respect the boundaries of others. This means listening to and acknowledging the needs and desires of others, and being willing to compromise and negotiate when necessary.

– Practice self-care: Taking care of yourself is an important aspect of setting and maintaining healthy boundaries. This may involve setting aside time for yourself, engaging in activities that bring you joy and relaxation, or seeking the help of a therapist or coach if you are struggling to set and maintain boundaries.

By following these tips, you can learn to set and maintain healthy boundaries in your relationships, and build healthier, more fulfilling connections with yourself and others. Remember, setting and respecting boundaries is an ongoing process, and it may take time and effort to develop healthy habits. Be patient with yourself, and seek help if you need it. With time, effort, and the right support, you can learn to set and maintain healthy boundaries and build stronger, more autonomous relationships.

In addition to setting and maintaining healthy boundaries, finding empowerment also involves developing a sense of self-worth and self-sufficiency. This may involve learning to rely on yourself for validation and support, rather than seeking these things from others. It may also involve practicing self-compassion and treating yourself with kindness and understanding, rather than judging or criticizing yourself.

By building self-worth and self-sufficiency, you can increase your sense of autonomy and self-reliance, and become more resilient in the face of challenges. This can also help you to build healthier, more fulfilling relationships, as you are less likely to rely on others for validation and support, and more likely to be able to stand up for yourself and assert your needs and desires.

Finally, breaking the cycle of co-dependency involves building healthier, more fulfilling relationships with others. This may involve learning how to communicate effectively, setting and respecting boundaries, and building trust and emotional intimacy. By cultivating these skills, you can build stronger, more fulfilling onnections with others, and create a more satisfying and self-sufficient life.

There are a few key strategies that can help you to break the cycle of co-dependency and build healthier, more fulfilling relationships:

– Seek therapy: Working with a trained therapist can be a valuable resource for individuals who want to explore co-dependent patterns of behavior and learn new ways of relating to others. Therapy can provide a safe and supportive space to process and work through difficult emotions, and to develop new coping strategies and patterns of behavior.

– Join a support group: Support groups can be a helpful resource for individuals who are working to overcome co-dependency. These groups provide a space to connect with others who are also struggling with similar challenges, and to learn from each other's experiences and insights.

– Read self-help books and materials: There are many self-help books and materials available that can provide guidance and support for individuals who are working to overcome co-dependent behavior. Reading about the experiences of others and learning about effective strategies for change can be a valuable resource on your journey of recovery.

– Practice healthy communication: Effective communication is an important aspect of building healthy, fulfilling relationships. This may involve learning how to express your

needs and desires in a clear and direct way, as well as listening to and acknowledging the needs of others.

By taking these steps and incorporating these strategies into
your life, you can break the cycle of co-dependency and
build healthier, more fulfilling relationships. Remember,
overcoming co-dependency is a journey that requires patience, self-compassion, and a commitment to personal
growth. With time, effort, and the right support, you can
create a more fulfilling and self-sufficient life for yourself.

In conclusion, breaking the cycle of co-dependency and
finding empowerment is a challenging but ultimately rewarding process. It involves learning how to set and maintain healthy boundaries, developing a sense of self-worth
and self-sufficiency, and building healthier, more fulfilling
relationships. While it may take time and effort, the benefits
of breaking the cycle of co-dependency are numerous, including increased well-being, improved mental health, and
stronger, more fulfilling relationships.

There are many resources available to help you on your
journey of overcoming co-dependency and finding empowerment. These may include therapy, support groups,

self-help books and materials, and healthy communication strategies. By seeking help and support, practicing self-care, and being patient with yourself, you can increase your chances of success in overcoming co-dependency and building a more fulfilling and self-sufficient life.

Remember, overcoming co-dependency is a journey that requires patience, self-compassion, and a commitment to personal growth. It may take time and effort to identify and address co-dependent behaviors, and there may be setbacks along the way. However, by seeking help and support, practicing self-care, and being patient with yourself, you can increase your chances of success in overcoming co-dependency and building healthier relationships. With the right support and a commitment to personal growth, you can break the cycle of co-dependency and create a more fulfilling and healthy life for yourself.

It is important to keep in mind that overcoming co-dependency and building healthier, more fulfilling relationships is a journey that requires time and effort, and there may be setbacks along the way. It is normal to feel overwhelmed or unsure at times, and it is important to be patient with yourself and to seek help if you need it.

Here are a few tips to help you stay motivated and on track as you work to overcome co-dependency and build healthier, more fulfilling relationships:

– Set goals and celebrate small victories: Setting small, achievable goals can help you to stay motivated and make progress on your journey of recovery. As you achieve each goal, take time to celebrate your progress and reward yourself for your efforts.

– Find a support network: Connecting with others who are also working to overcome co-dependency or who have overcome similar challenges can provide a sense of connection and support. Consider joining a support group or connecting with a coach or therapist who can provide guidance and encouragement.

– Practice self-care: Taking care of yourself is an important aspect of overcoming co-dependency and building healthier, more fulfilling relationships. Make time for activities that bring you joy and relaxation, and seek the help of a therapist or coach if you are struggling to cope with difficult emotions.

— Seek out healthy role models or mentors: Having someone to look up to or to provide guidance and inspiration can be an important aspect of personal growth and healing. Consider seeking out a mentor or role model who has overcome similar challenges and can offer guidance and support as you work to build a more fulfilling life.

By following these tips and seeking the right support, you can stay motivated and on track as you work to overcome co-dependency and build healthier, more fulfilling relationships. Remember, overcoming co-dependency is a journey that requires patience, self-compassion, and a commitment to personal growth. With the right support and a commitment to change, you can build a more fulfilling and healthy life for yourself.

06: The Role of Communication in Overcoming Co-dependency

Effective communication is an essential component of healthy, fulfilling relationships, and it can play a vital role in overcoming co-dependency. Co-dependent relationships are often characterized by unhealthy patterns of communication, including codependent behavior, lack of assertiveness, and an inability to express needs and boundaries. By learning how to communicate effectively, individuals can break the cycle of co-dependency and build healthier, more autonomous relationships.

So, what does effective communication look like, and how can it help you to overcome co-dependency?

– Assertiveness: Assertiveness involves being able to express your own needs and desires in a clear and direct way, without being aggressive or submissive. It involves being able to stand up for yourself and your beliefs, and to communicate your boundaries in a healthy and respectful way. Assertiveness can be an important aspect of overcoming co-dependency, as it allows you to express your own needs and desires, rather than relying on others for validation or support.

06: THE ROLE OF COMMUNICATION IN OVERCOMING CO-DEPENDENCY

– Active listening: Active listening involves fully paying attention to what the other person is saying, and making an effort to understand their perspective. It involves asking questions, clarifying, and showing empathy. Active listening can be an important aspect of overcoming co-dependency, as it allows you to better understand the needs and perspectives of others, and to build trust and emotional intimacy.

– Clear and direct communication: Clear and direct communication involves being able to express your thoughts and feelings in a clear and concise way, without being passive or aggressive. It involves being honest and open, and being able to communicate your needs and boundaries in a healthy and respectful way. Clear and direct communication can be an important aspect of overcoming co-dependency, as it allows you to express your needs and boundaries, and to build healthier, more fulfilling relationships.

By incorporating these elements of effective communication into your relationships, you can begin to break the cycle of co-dependency and build healthier, more autonomous connections with others. Remember, effective communication is an ongoing process, and it may take time and effort to develop healthy habits. Be patient with yourself, and seek help if you need it. With time, effort, and the right support, you can learn to communicate effectively and build stronger, more fulfilling relationships.

In addition to assertiveness, active listening, and clear and direct communication, there are a few other strategies that can be helpful in overcoming co-dependency and building healthier relationships:

– Seek therapy: Working with a trained therapist can be a valuable resource for individuals who want to explore co-dependent patterns of behavior and learn new ways of relating to others. Therapy can provide a safe and supportive space to process and work through difficult emotions, and to develop new coping strategies and patterns of behavior.

– Join a support group: Support groups can be a helpful resource for individuals who are working to overcome co-dependency. These groups provide a space to connect with others who are also struggling with similar challenges, and to learn from each other's experiences and insights.

06: THE ROLE OF COMMUNICATION IN OVERCOMING CO-DEPENDENCY

– Practice self-care: Taking care of yourself is an important aspect of overcoming co-dependency and building healthier, more fulfilling relationships. Make time for activities that bring you joy and relaxation, and seek the help of a therapist or coach if you are struggling to cope with difficult emotions.

– Seek out healthy role models or mentors: Having someone to look up to or to provide guidance and inspiration can be an important aspect of personal growth and healing. Consider seeking out a mentor or role model who has overcome similar challenges and can offer guidance and support as you work to build a more fulfilling life.

By incorporating these strategies into your life, you can increase your chances of success in overcoming co-dependency and building healthier, more fulfilling relationships. Remember, overcoming co-dependency is a journey that requires patience, self-compassion, and a commitment to personal growth. With the right support and a commitment to change, you can build a more fulfilling and healthy life for yourself.

In conclusion, effective communication is an essential component of healthy, fulfilling relationships, and it can play a vital role in overcoming co-dependency. Assertiveness, active listening, and clear and direct communication are all important aspects of effective communication that can help you to build stronger, more autonomous relationships.

There are also a number of resources available to help you learn and practice effective communication skills. These may include therapy, support groups, self-help books and materials, and healthy communication strategies. By seeking help and support, practicing self-care, and being patient with yourself, you can increase your chances of success in overcoming co-dependency and building healthier, more fulfilling relationships.

Remember, overcoming co-dependency is a journey that requires patience, self-compassion, and a commitment to personal growth. It may take time and effort to identify and address co-dependent behaviors, and there may be setbacks along the way. However, by seeking help and support, practicing self-care, and being patient with yourself, you can increase your chances of success in overcoming co-dependency and building healthier relationships. With the right

support and a commitment to change, you can build a more
fulfilling and healthy life for yourself.

It is important to remember that overcoming co-dependency and building healthier, more fulfilling relationships is
a journey that requires time and effort, and there may be
setbacks along the way. It is normal to feel overwhelmed or
unsure at times, and it is important to be patient with yourself and to seek help if you need it.

Here are a few tips to help you stay motivated and on track
as you work to overcome co-dependency and build healthier, more fulfilling relationships:

– Set goals and celebrate small victories: Setting small,
achievable goals can help you to stay motivated and make
progress on your journey of recovery. As you achieve each
goal, take time to celebrate your progress and reward yourself for your efforts.

– Find a support network: Connecting with others who are
also working to overcome co-dependency or who have overcome similar challenges can provide a sense of connection
and support. Consider joining a support group or connect-

ing with a coach or therapist who can provide guidance and encouragement.

– Practice self-care: Taking care of yourself is an important aspect of overcoming co-dependency and building healthier, more fulfilling relationships. Make time for activities that bring you joy and relaxation, and seek the help of a therapist or coach if you are struggling to cope with difficult emotions.

– Seek out healthy role models or mentors: Having someone to look up to or to provide guidance and inspiration can be an important aspect of personal growth and healing. Consider seeking out a mentor or role model who has overcome similar challenges and can offer guidance and support as you work to build a more fulfilling life.

By following these tips and seeking the right support, you can stay motivated and on track as you work to overcome co-dependency and build healthier, more fulfilling relationships. Remember, overcoming co-dependency is a journey that requires patience, self-compassion, and a commitment to personal growth. With the right support and a commitment to change, you can build a more fulfilling and healthy life for yourself.

07: Healing from Childhood Trauma: Techniques and Strategies

Childhood trauma can have a lasting impact on an individual's mental health and well-being. It can manifest as a wide range of physical, emotional, and behavioral symptoms, including difficulty with relationships, low self-esteem, and a lack of trust in others. Healing from childhood trauma is a complex and often difficult process, but it is possible with the right support and strategies.

Here are a few techniques and strategies that may be helpful in healing from childhood trauma:

– Seek therapy: Working with a trained therapist can be a valuable resource for individuals who want to explore and heal from their childhood trauma. Therapy can provide a safe and supportive space to process and work through difficult emotions, and to develop coping strategies and patterns of behavior.

– Practice self-care: Taking care of yourself is an important aspect of healing from childhood trauma. This may involve setting aside time for yourself, engaging in activities that

bring you joy and relaxation, or seeking the help of a therapist or coach if you are struggling to cope with difficult
emotions.

– Connect with others: Connecting with others who have
experienced similar challenges can be a valuable resource
for healing from childhood trauma. Consider joining a support group or connecting with a coach or therapist who can
provide guidance and encouragement.

– Practice mindfulness: Mindfulness involves paying attention to the present moment, without judgment. It can be an
effective tool for coping with difficult emotions and managing stress. There are many resources available to help you
learn mindfulness techniques, including books, apps, and
therapy.

– Seek out healthy role models or mentors: Having
someone to look up to or to provide guidance and inspiration can be an important aspect of personal growth and
healing. Consider seeking out a mentor or role model who
has overcome similar challenges and can offer guidance and
support as you work to heal from your childhood trauma.

07: HEALING FROM CHILDHOOD TRAUMA: TECHNIQUES AND STRATEGIES

By incorporating these strategies into your life, you can increase your chances of success in healing from childhood trauma and building a more fulfilling and healthy life for yourself. Remember, healing from childhood trauma is a journey that requires patience, self-compassion, and a commitment to personal growth. With the right support and a commitment to change, you can build a more fulfilling and healthy life for yourself.

It is important to keep in mind that healing from childhood trauma is a complex and often difficult process, and it may take time and effort to make progress. It is normal to feel overwhelmed or unsure at times, and it is important to be patient with yourself and to seek help if you need it.

Here are a few additional tips to help you stay motivated and on track as you work to heal from childhood trauma:

– Set goals and celebrate small victories: Setting small, achievable goals can help you to stay motivated and make progress on your journey of recovery. As you achieve each goal, take time to celebrate your progress and reward yourself for your efforts.

07: HEALING FROM CHILDHOOD TRAUMA: TECH-NIQUES AND STRATEGIES

– Practice self-compassion: Self-compassion involves being kind and understanding towards yourself, especially during difficult times. It involves acknowledging that everyone makes mistakes and experiences suffering, and that it is okay to ask for help. Practicing self-compassion can be an important aspect of healing from childhood trauma, as it can help you to build self-acceptance and resilience.

– Find healthy ways to cope with difficult emotions: Healing from childhood trauma often involves learning how to cope with difficult emotions in healthy ways. This may involve practicing mindfulness, engaging in self-care activities, or finding healthy outlets for stress, such as exercise or hobbies.

– Build a supportive network: Building a network of supportive people can be an important aspect of healing from childhood trauma. Consider reaching out to trusted friends and family members, or connecting with others who have experienced similar challenges.

By following these tips and seeking the right support, you can stay motivated and on track as you work to heal from childhood trauma and build a more fulfilling and healthy life for yourself. Remember, healing from childhood trauma is a journey that requires patience, self compassion, and a commitment to personal growth. It may take time and effort to make progress, and there may be setbacks along the way. However, by seeking help and support, practicing self-care, and being patient with yourself, you can increase your chances of success in healing from childhood trauma and building a more fulfilling and healthy life for yourself.

It is also important to keep in mind that healing from childhood trauma is not a linear process, and it may involve ups and downs. It is normal to feel a range of emotions as you work through your trauma, and it is important to be kind and understanding towards yourself, especially during difficult times.

It may also be helpful to remember that you are not alone in your journey of healing from childhood trauma. There are many resources and support systems available to help you, including therapy, support groups, and self-help materials. By seeking out the right help and support, you can increase your chances of success in healing from childhood trauma and building a more fulfilling and healthy life for yourself.

In conclusion, healing from childhood trauma is a complex and often difficult process, but it is possible with the right support and strategies. Techniques such as therapy, self-care, connecting with others, practicing mindfulness, and seeking out healthy role models or mentors can all be helpful in healing from childhood trauma and building a more fulfilling and healthy life for yourself.

It is important to remember that healing from childhood trauma is a journey that requires patience, self-compassion, and a commitment to personal growth. It may take time and effort to make progress, and there may be setbacks along the way. However, by seeking help and support, practicing self-care, and being patient with yourself, you can increase your chances of success in healing from childhood trauma and building a more fulfilling and healthy life for yourself.

Remember, you are not alone in your journey of healing from childhood trauma. There are many resources and support systems available to help you, including therapy, support groups, and self-help materials. By seeking out the right help and support, you can increase your chances of success in healing from childhood trauma and building a more fulfilling and healthy life for yourself.

08: Building a Support System for Recovery

Building a support system is an important aspect of recovery from any challenge, including co-dependency, childhood trauma, or other mental health issues. A support system can provide a sense of connection and belonging, as well as practical and emotional support during difficult times. It can also be an important source of motivation and encouragement as you work to build a more fulfilling and healthy life for yourself.

So, how can you go about building a support system for recovery? Here are a few tips to get you started:

– Identify your needs: The first step in building a support system is to identify your needs. This may include emotional support, practical support, or a combination of both. Think about what you need to feel supported and fulfilled, and make a list of the types of support you are looking for.

– Reach out to trusted friends and family members: Your friends and family can be an important source of support and connection. Consider reaching out to trusted friends and family members to see if they are willing to provide the types of support you are looking for. This could involve having someone to talk to, asking for practical help with tasks or errands, or simply having someone to spend time with.

– Join a support group: Support groups can be a helpful resource for individuals who are working to overcome challenges and build healthier, more fulfilling lives. These groups provide a space to connect with others who are also struggling with similar challenges, and to learn from each other's experiences and insights.

– Seek out a mentor or role model: Having someone to look up to or to provide guidance and inspiration can be an important aspect of personal growth and healing. Consider seeking out a mentor or role model who has overcome similar challenges and can offer guidance and support as you work to build a more fulfilling life.

– Consider seeking professional help: If you are struggling to cope with difficult emotions or to build a supportive network, consider seeking the help of a trained therapist or coach. These professionals can provide a safe and supportive space to explore your feelings and develop coping strategies and patterns of behavior.

By incorporating these strategies into your life, you can build a support system that can help you to recover from challenges and build a more fulfilling and healthy life for yourself. Remember, building a support system is an ongoing process, and it may take time and effort to develop healthy habits. Be patient with yourself, and seek help if you need it. With time, effort, and the right support, you can build a strong and supportive network that can help you to recover from challenges and build a more fulfilling and healthy life for yourself.

Here are a few additional tips for building and maintaining a support system for recovery:

– Be open and honest about your needs: In order for your support system to be effective, it is important to be open and honest about your needs. This may involve communicating your feelings and needs to your friends and family, or seeking out a therapist or coach who can provide a safe and supportive space to explore your feelings.

– Practice gratitude: Focusing on the things you are grateful for can help to shift your perspective and build a sense of connection and appreciation. Consider keeping a gratitude journal or sharing your gratitude with others in your support system.

– Take care of yourself: Taking care of yourself is an important aspect of building and maintaining a support system for recovery. Make time for activities that bring you joy and relaxation, and seek the help of a therapist or coach if you are struggling to cope with difficult emotions.

– Seek out new connections: Building a support system is an ongoing process, and it can be helpful to seek out new connections and opportunities for support. This may involve joining a new group or club, or volunteering your time to help others.

– Remember that it is okay to ask for help: Asking for help is a sign of strength, not weakness. If you are struggling to cope with difficult emotions or to build a supportive network, it is important to remember that it is okay to ask for help. There are many resources and support systems available to help you, including therapy, support groups, and self-help materials.

By following these tips and seeking the right support, you can build and maintain a strong and supportive network that can help you to recover from challenges and build a more fulfilling and healthy life for yourself. Remember, building a support system is an ongoing process, and it may take time and effort to develop healthy habits. Be patient with yourself, and seek help if you need it. With time, effort, and the right support, you can build a strong and supportive network that can help you to recover from challenges and build a more fulfilling and healthy life for yourself.

In conclusion, building and maintaining a support system is an important aspect of recovery from any challenge, including co-dependency, childhood trauma, or other mental health issues. A support system can provide a sense of connection and belonging, as well as practical and emotional support during difficult times. It can also be an important source of motivation and encouragement as you work to build a more fulfilling and healthy life for yourself.

There are many ways to build and maintain a support system for recovery, including reaching out to trusted friends and family members, joining a support group, seeking out a mentor or role model, and seeking professional help. It is also important to be open and honest about your needs, practice gratitude, take care of yourself, seek out new connections, and remember that it is okay to ask for help.

Building a support system is an ongoing process, and it may take time and effort to develop healthy habits. Be patient with yourself, and seek help if you need it. With time, effort, and the right support, you can build a strong and supportive network that can help you to recover from challenges and build a more fulfilling and healthy life for yourself.

It is also important to keep in mind that building and maintaining a support system is an ongoing process, and it may involve making adjustments and changes over time. It is normal to experience ups and downs, and to need different levels of support at different times. It is important to be flexible and adaptable, and to be open to seeking out new sources of support as needed.

Here are a few additional tips for building and maintaining a strong and supportive network:

– Cultivate healthy relationships: Building and maintaining healthy relationships is an important aspect of a supportive network. This may involve setting boundaries, communicating openly and honestly, and showing appreciation and gratitude towards others.

– Practice active listening: Active listening involves paying attention to what others are saying and responding with understanding and empathy. It is an important aspect of building and maintaining healthy relationships, and can help to foster a sense of connection and support.

– Offer support and encouragement: A supportive network is not just about receiving support, but also about giving support and encouragement to others. Consider ways in which you can offer support and encouragement to others in your network, whether it be through words of encouragement, a listening ear, or practical help.

– Seek out new connections and opportunities: Building and maintaining a supportive network is an ongoing process, and it can be helpful to seek out new connections and opportunities for support. This may involve joining a new group or club, or volunteering your time to help others.

By following these tips and seeking the right support, you can build and maintain a strong and supportive network that can help you to recover from challenges and build a more fulfilling and healthy life for yourself. Remember, building and maintaining a support system is an ongoing process, and it may take time and effort to develop healthy habits. Be patient with yourself, and seek help if you need it. With time, effort, and the right support, you can build a strong and supportive network that can help you to recover from challenges and build a more fulfilling and healthy life for yourself.

It is also important to remember that a supportive network is not just about seeking help and support from others, but also about taking care of yourself and building resilience. Building resilience involves developing the skills and coping strategies needed to cope with difficult situations and emotions, and to bounce back from setbacks and challenges. Some strategies for building resilience include:

– Practicing self-care: Taking care of yourself is an important aspect of building resilience. This may involve setting aside time for yourself, engaging in activities that bring you joy and relaxation, or seeking the help of a therapist or coach if you are struggling to cope with difficult emotions.

– Developing a support network: Building and maintaining a supportive network of friends, family, and other trusted individuals can be an important aspect of building resilience. A supportive network can provide a sense of connection and belonging, as well as practical and emotional support during difficult times.

– Seeking professional help: If you are struggling to cope with difficult emotions or to build a supportive network, consider seeking the help of a trained therapist or coach. These professionals can provide a safe and supportive space to explore your feelings and develop coping strategies and patterns of behavior.

– Practicing mindfulness: Mindfulness involves paying attention to the present moment, without judgment. It can be an effective tool for coping with difficult emotions and building resilience. There are many resources available to help you learn mindfulness techniques, including books, apps, and therapy.

– Setting goals and celebrating progress: Setting small, achievable goals can help you to stay motivated and make progress on your journey of recovery. As you achieve each goal, take time to celebrate your progress and reward yourself for your efforts.

By incorporating these strategies into your life, you can

build resilience and increase your chances of success in re-covering from challenges and building a more fulfilling and healthy life for yourself. Remember, building resilience is an ongoing process, and it may take time and effort to develop healthy habits. Be patient with yourself, and seek help if you need it. With time, effort, and the right support, you can build resilience and increase your chances of success in re-covering from challenges and building a more fulfilling and healthy life for yourself.

It is also important to keep in mind that building resilience is not about being able to handle everything on your own, or about pretending that you don't need help or support. Instead, it is about developing the skills and coping strategies needed to cope with difficult situations and emotions, and to bounce back from setbacks and challenges. This may involve seeking help and support from others when needed, and being open and honest about your needs and feelings.

Finally, it is important to remember that building resilience is not about being perfect or never experiencing setbacks or challenges. It is about developing the skills and coping strategies needed to cope with difficult situations and emo-tions, and to bounce back from setbacks and challenges. It is a journey that requires patience, self-compassion, and a commitment to personal growth. With time, effort, and the right support, you can build resilience and increase your chances of success in recovering from challenges and building a more fulfilling and healthy life for yourself.

09: Finding Self-worth and Self-love in Recovery

Finding self-worth and self-love is an important aspect of recovery from any challenge, including co-dependency, childhood trauma, or other mental health issues. Self-worth is a belief in your own value and worth as a person, while self-love is an acceptance and appreciation of yourself, including your strengths and weaknesses. Developing self-worth and self-love can be a challenging process, but it is an important step towards building a more fulfilling and healthy life for yourself.

So, how can you go about finding self-worth and self-love in recovery? Here are a few tips to get you started:

– Practice self-acceptance: Self-acceptance involves accepting and embracing yourself as you are, including your strengths and weaknesses. It is an important aspect of developing self-worth and self-love, and can be challenging for many people, especially those who have experienced trauma or other challenges. One way to practice self-acceptance is to focus on your positive qualities and to remind yourself that it is okay to have weaknesses and to make mistakes.

09: FINDING SELF-WORTH AND SELF-LOVE IN RE-COVERY

– Seek out positive role models and mentors: Having someone to look up to or to provide guidance and inspiration can be an important aspect of personal growth and self-love. Consider seeking out positive role models or mentors who embody the qualities you admire, and who can offer guidance and support as you work to build a more fulfilling and healthy life for yourself.

– Engage in self-care: Taking care of yourself is an important aspect of building self-worth and self-love. This may involve setting aside time for yourself, engaging in activities that bring you joy and relaxation, or seeking the help of a therapist or coach if you are struggling to cope with difficult emotions.

– Practice gratitude: Focusing on the things you are grateful for can help to shift your perspective and build a sense of appreciation and self-worth. Consider keeping a gratitude journal or sharing your gratitude with others in your support system.

– Seek professional help: If you are struggling to cope with difficult emotions or to build self-worth and self-love, consider seeking the help of a trained therapist or coach. These professionals can provide a safe and supportive space to explore your feelings and develop coping strategies and patterns of behavior.

By incorporating these strategies into your life, you can build self-worth and self-love and increase your chances of success in recovering from challenges and building a more fulfilling and healthy life for yourself. Remember, finding self-worth and self-love is a journey that requires patience, self-compassion, and a commitment to personal growth. It may take time and effort to make progress, and there may be setbacks along the way. However, with time, effort, and the right support, you can build self-worth and self-love and increase your chances of success in recovering from challenges and building a more fulfilling and healthy life for yourself.

Here are a few additional tips for finding self-worth and self-love in recovery:

– Seek out new experiences and challenges: Engaging in new experiences and challenges can help you to grow and develop new skills, which can in turn boost your self-worth and self-love. Consider trying new hobbies or activities, or seeking out new opportunities for personal growth and development.

– Practice self-compassion: Self-compassion involves treating yourself with kindness and understanding, rather than judgment or criticism. It is an important aspect of self-love, and can be a powerful tool for coping with difficult emotions and setbacks.

– Set boundaries: Setting boundaries involves establishing clear and healthy limits with others, and taking care of your own needs and well-being. It is an important aspect of self-worth and self-love, and can help you to feel more in control of your life and more empowered.

– Find your passions and purpose: Discovering your passions and purpose can be an important aspect of building self-worth and self-love. Consider what brings you joy and fulfillment, and seek out opportunities to pursue these passions and to make a positive impact in the world.

It is also important to keep in mind that finding self-worth and self-love is not about achieving perfection or never experiencing setbacks or challenges. It is about developing a healthy and positive sense of self-worth and self-love, and about embracing and accepting yourself as you are, flaws and all. It is a journey that requires patience, self-compassion, and a commitment to personal growth.

Here are a few additional tips for finding self-worth and self-love in recovery:

– Seek out supportive relationships: Building and maintaining supportive relationships with friends, family, and other trusted individuals can be an important aspect of building self-worth and self-love. A supportive network can provide a sense of connection and belonging, as well as practical and emotional support during difficult times.

– Practice gratitude: Focusing on the things you are grateful for can help to shift your perspective and build a sense of appreciation and self-worth. Consider keeping a gratitude journal or sharing your gratitude with others in your support system.

– Take care of your physical health: Taking care of your physical health is an important aspect of building self-worth and self-love. This may involve exercising regularly, eating a healthy and balanced diet, and getting enough sleep.

– Seek out new opportunities for personal growth: Personal growth is an important aspect of building self-worth and self-love. Consider seeking out new opportunities for personal growth, such as learning a new skill, taking on a new challenge, or pursuing a new hobby or activity.

It is also important to remember that finding self-worth and self-love is not just about focusing on your own needs and well-being, but also about being a part of something larger than yourself. Engaging in activities and causes that are meaningful to you and that make a positive impact in the world can be an important aspect of building self-worth and self-love. This may involve volunteering your time or resources, or advocating for causes you care about.

– Practice gratitude: Focusing on the things you are grateful for can help to shift your perspective and build a sense of appreciation and self-worth. Consider keeping a gratitude journal or sharing your gratitude with others in your support system.

– Seek out supportive relationships: Building and maintaining supportive relationships with friends, family, and other trusted individuals can be an important aspect of building self-worth and self-love. A supportive network can provide a sense of connection and belonging, as well as practical and emotional support during difficult times.

– Seek out new opportunities for personal growth: Personal growth is an important aspect of building self-worth and self-love. Consider seeking out new opportunities for personal growth, such as learning a new skill, taking on a new challenge, or pursuing a new hobby or activity.

– Engage in activities and causes that are meaningful to you: Engaging in activities and causes that are meaningful to you and that make a positive impact in the world can be an important aspect of building self-worth and self-love. This may involve volunteering your time or resources, or advocating for causes you care about.

It is also important to remember that building self-worth and self-love is not a solo journey. Seeking the help and support of others, whether through therapy, support groups, or other resources, can be an important aspect of building self-worth and self-love. These resources can provide a safe and supportive space to explore your feelings and develop coping strategies and patterns of behavior.

Here are a few additional tips for finding self-worth and self-love in recovery:

– Practice self-compassion: Self-compassion involves treating yourself with kindness and understanding, rather than judgment or criticism. It is an important aspect of self-love, and can be a powerful tool for coping with difficult emotions and setbacks.

– Set boundaries: Setting boundaries involves establishing clear and healthy limits with others, and taking care of your own needs and well-being. It is an important aspect of self-worth and self-love, and can help you to feel more in control of your life and more empowered.

– Seek out new experiences and challenges: Engaging in new experiences and challenges can help you to grow and develop new skills, which can in turn boost your self-worth and self-love. Consider trying new hobbies or activities, or seeking out new opportunities for personal growth and development.

09: FINDING SELF-WORTH AND SELF-LOVE IN RE-COVERY

– Seek out supportive relationships: Building and maintaining supportive relationships with friends, family, and other trusted individuals can be an important aspect of building self-worth and self-love. A supportive network can provide a sense of connection and belonging, as well as practical and emotional support during difficult times.

By following these tips and seeking the right support, you can build self-worth and self-love and increase your chances of success in recovering from challenges and building a more fulfilling and healthy life for yourself. Remember, finding self-worth and self-love is a journey that requires patience, self-compassion, and a commitment to personal growth. It may take time and effort to make progress, and there may be setbacks along the way. However, with time, effort, and the right support, you can build self-worth and self-love and increase your chances of success in recovering from challenges and building a more fulfilling and healthy life for yourself.

10: Navigating Intimate Relationships in Recovery

Navigating intimate relationships can be a challenging aspect of recovery from any challenge, including co-dependency, childhood trauma, or other mental health issues. Building and maintaining healthy and fulfilling intimate relationships requires a strong sense of self-worth and self-love, as well as good communication and relationship skills. It is important to be honest with yourself and with your partner about your needs and boundaries, and to be open to seeking help and support if needed.

So, how can you navigate intimate relationships in recovery? Here are a few tips to get you started:

– Practice self-acceptance: Self-acceptance involves accepting and embracing yourself as you are, including your strengths and weaknesses. It is an important aspect of building self-worth and self-love, and can be challenging for many people, especially those who have experienced trauma or other challenges. One way to practice self-acceptance is to focus on your positive qualities and to remind yourself that it is okay to have weaknesses and to make mistakes.

– Communicate openly and honestly: Good communication is an important aspect of any healthy relationship. It is important to be open and honest with your partner about your needs, boundaries, and feelings, and to listen actively to your partner's perspective. Seek out resources, such as therapy or communication workshops, if you are struggling with communication in your relationship.

– Set boundaries: Setting boundaries involves establishing clear and healthy limits with your partner, and taking care of your own needs and well-being. It is an important aspect of self-worth and self-love, and can help you to feel more in control of your life and more empowered.

– Seek out support: If you are struggling to navigate your intimate relationships, consider seeking the help of a trained therapist or coach. These professionals can provide a safe and supportive space to explore your feelings and develop coping strategies and patterns of behavior.

It is also important to remember that building and maintaining healthy and fulfilling intimate relationships is not about achieving perfection or never experiencing setbacks or challenges. It is about developing healthy patterns of behavior and communication, and about embracing and accepting yourself and your partner as you are, flaws and all. It is a journey that requires patience, self-compassion, and a commitment to personal growth.

One way to build and maintain healthy and fulfilling intimate relationships is to practice forgiveness. Forgiveness is an important aspect of building and maintaining healthy and fulfilling relationships. It involves letting go of anger and resentment, and focusing on the positive aspects of your relationship. Practicing forgiveness can be challenging, but it can also be incredibly freeing and can help you to build a more positive and healthy relationship with your partner.

Another way to navigate intimate relationships in recovery is to seek out new experiences and challenges. Engaging in new experiences and challenges can help you to grow and develop new skills, which can in turn boost your self-worth and self-love. Consider trying new hobbies or activities, or seeking out new opportunities for personal growth and development.

Building a strong support network is also an important aspect of navigating intimate relationships in recovery. A strong support network of friends, family, and other trusted individuals can provide a sense of connection and belonging, as well as practical and emotional support during difficult times. Consider reaching out to your support network for help and guidance when you are struggling with your intimate relationships.

Finally, seeking out therapy or coaching can be an effective way to navigate intimate relationships in recovery. If you are struggling to navigate your intimate relationships, consider seeking the help of a trained therapist or coach. These professionals can provide a safe and supportive space to explore your feelings and develop coping strategies and patterns of behavior.

It is also important to remember that building and maintaining healthy and fulfilling intimate relationships requires a commitment to ongoing learning and growth. This may involve seeking out new resources, such as books, workshops, or therapy, to learn more about healthy relationship patterns and communication skills. It may also involve being open to feedback from your partner and other trusted individuals, and being willing to make changes in your behavior as needed.

Here are a few additional tips for navigating intimate relationships in recovery:

– Practice self-care: Taking care of your own needs and well-being is an important aspect of building and maintaining healthy and fulfilling relationships. This may involve setting aside time for yourself, engaging in activities that bring you joy and fulfillment, and seeking out the support you need when you are struggling.

– Seek out new experiences and challenges: Engaging in new experiences and challenges can help you to grow and develop new skills, which can in turn boost your self-worth and self-love. Consider trying new hobbies or activities, or seeking out new opportunities for personal growth and development.

– Build a strong support network: A strong support network of friends, family, and other trusted individuals can provide a sense of connection and belonging, as well as practical and emotional support during difficult times. Consider reaching out to your support network for help and guidance when you are struggling with your intimate relationships.

– Seek out therapy or coaching: If you are struggling to navigate your intimate relationships, consider seeking the help of a trained therapist or coach. These professionals can provide a safe and supportive space to explore your feelings and develop coping strategies and patterns of behavior.

– Seek out healthy role models: Observing and learning from healthy relationships can be a helpful way to develop your own skills and patterns of behavior. Consider seeking out healthy role models, such as friends or family members who have strong and fulfilling relationships, and observing and learning from their communication and relationship patterns.

– Practice gratitude: Practicing gratitude involves focusing on the positive aspects of your life, including your relationships. It can help to shift your perspective and to cultivate a sense of contentment and well-being. Consider starting a gratitude journal or sharing your gratitude with your partner on a regular basis.

– Seek out relationship education: There are many re-

sources available to help you learn more about healthy relationship patterns and communication skills. Consider seeking out books, workshops, or therapy to learn more about
how to build and maintain healthy and fulfilling relationships.

– Practice self-compassion: Self-compassion involves being
kind and understanding towards yourself, especially during
difficult times. It can be helpful in building and maintaining
healthy and fulfilling relationships, as it allows you to be
more understanding and forgiving towards yourself and
your partner.

It is also important to remember that building and maintaining healthy and fulfilling intimate relationships requires
a commitment to ongoing learning and growth. This may
involve seeking out new resources, such as books, workshops, or therapy, to learn more about healthy relationship
patterns and communication skills. It may also involve being open to feedback from your partner and other trusted
individuals, and being willing to make changes in your behavior as needed.

– Practice healthy communication: Effective communication is an important aspect of any healthy relationship. It involves being open and honest with your partner about your needs, boundaries, and feelings, and listening actively to your partner's perspective. Seek out resources, such as therapy or communication workshops, if you are struggling with communication in your relationship.

– Seek out relationship education: There are many resources available to help you learn more about healthy relationship patterns and communication skills. Consider seeking out books, workshops, or therapy to learn more about how to build and maintain healthy and fulfilling relationships.

– Practice forgiveness: Forgiveness is an important aspect of building and maintaining healthy and fulfilling relationships. It involves letting go of anger and resentment, and focusing on the positive aspects of your relationship. Practicing forgiveness can be challenging, but it can also be incredibly freeing and can help you to build a more positive and healthy relationship with your partner.

– Seek out therapy or coaching: If you are struggling to navigate your intimate relationships, consider seeking the help of a trained therapist or coach. These professionals can provide a safe and supportive space to explore your feelings and develop coping strategies and patterns of behavior.

By following these tips and seeking the right support, you can navigate intimate relationships in recovery and build a more fulfilling and healthy life for yourself. Remember, building and maintaining healthy and fulfilling intimate relationships is a journey that requires patience, self-compassion, and a commitment to personal growth. It may take time and effort to make progress, and there may be setbacks along the way. However, with time, effort, and the right support, you can navigate intimate relationships in recovery and build a more fulfilling and healthy life for yourself.

11: Coping with Triggers and Relapses

Triggers and relapses are common challenges that many people face in their journey towards recovery from co-dependency, childhood trauma, or other mental health issues. A trigger is anything that can cause a person to experience a strong emotional or physical reaction, often related to past trauma or negative experiences. A relapse refers to a return to old patterns of behavior or thinking, which can be triggered by certain events or circumstances.

Dealing with triggers and preventing relapses is an important part of the recovery process. Here are a few tips to help you cope with triggers and prevent relapses:

– Identify your triggers: The first step in coping with triggers is to become aware of what triggers you. This may involve reflecting on past experiences and the emotions or circumstances that led to a relapse or negative coping behaviors. Once you have identified your triggers, you can develop strategies for managing them.

– Develop a plan for managing triggers: Once you have identified your triggers, it is important to develop a plan for managing them. This may involve identifying healthy coping strategies, such as seeking support from friends or a therapist, practicing self-care, or using relaxation techniques. It may also involve identifying and avoiding situations or environments that may trigger a relapse.

– Build a strong support network: A strong support network of friends, family, and other trusted individuals can provide a sense of connection and belonging, as well as practical and emotional support during difficult times. Consider reaching out to your support network for help and guidance when you are struggling with triggers or at risk of a relapse.

– Seek out therapy or coaching: If you are struggling to cope with triggers or prevent relapses, consider seeking the help of a trained therapist or coach. These professionals can provide a safe and supportive space to explore your feelings and develop coping strategies and patterns of behavior.

– Practice self-compassion: Self-compassion involves being kind and understanding towards yourself, especially during difficult times. It can be helpful in coping with triggers and preventing relapses, as it allows you to be more understanding and forgiving towards yourself and your limitations.

By following these tips and seeking the right support, you can cope with triggers and prevent relapses in your journey towards recovery. Remember, dealing with triggers and preventing relapses is an ongoing process that requires patience, self-compassion, and a commitment to personal growth. It may take time and effort to make progress, and there may be setbacks along the way. However, with time, effort, and the right support, you can cope with triggers and prevent relapses and build a more fulfilling and healthy life for yourself.

Here are a few more tips for coping with triggers and preventing relapses:

– Practice mindfulness: Mindfulness is the practice of being present in the moment, without judgment. It can be a helpful tool in coping with triggers and preventing relapses, as it allows you to become more aware of your thoughts, feelings, and physical sensations, and to respond to them in a more healthy and balanced way.

– Seek out new experiences and challenges: Engaging in new experiences and challenges can help you to grow and develop new skills, which can in turn boost your self-worth and self-love. Consider trying new hobbies or activities, or seeking out new opportunities for personal growth and development.

– Practice self-care: Taking care of your own needs and well-being is an important aspect of coping with triggers and preventing relapses. This may involve setting aside time for yourself, engaging in activities that bring you joy and fulfillment, and seeking out the support you need when you are struggling.

– Seek out healthy role models: Observing and learning from healthy relationships can be a helpful way to develop your own skills and patterns of behavior. Consider seeking out healthy role models, such as friends or family members who have strong and fulfilling relationships, and observing and learning from their communication and relationship patterns.

– Seek out relationship education: There are many resources available to help you learn more about healthy relationship patterns and communication skills. Consider seeking out books, workshops, or therapy to learn more about how to build and maintain healthy and fulfilling relationships.

It is also important to remember that coping with triggers and preventing relapses is an ongoing process that requires a commitment to ongoing learning and growth. This may involve seeking out new resources, such as books, workshops, or therapy, to learn more about healthy coping strategies and relationship patterns. It may also involve being open to feedback from your support network and being willing to make changes in your behavior as needed.

Here are a few additional tips for coping with triggers and preventing relapses:

– Practice gratitude: Practicing gratitude involves focusing on the positive aspects of your life, including your relationships. It can help to shift your perspective and to cultivate a sense of contentment and well-being. Consider starting a gratitude journal or sharing your gratitude with your partner on a regular basis.

– Seek out new sources of support: In addition to your regular support network, there are many other resources available to help you cope with triggers and prevent relapses. These may include online support groups, helplines, and peer support programs. Consider seeking out new sources of support to help you navigate difficult times.

– Practice healthy communication: Effective communication is an important aspect of any healthy relationship. It involves being open and honest with your partner about your needs, boundaries, and feelings, and listening actively to your partner's perspective. Seek out resources, such as therapy or communication workshops, if you are struggling with communication in your relationship.

– Seek out new opportunities for personal growth and development: Engaging in new experiences and challenges can help you to grow and develop new skills, which can in turn boost your self-worth and self-love. Consider seeking out new opportunities for personal growth and development, such as workshops, classes, or volunteer work.

It is also important to remember that everyone's journey towards recovery is unique, and what works for one person may not work for another. It is important to be patient with yourself and to focus on your own progress and growth, rather than comparing yourself to others.

Here are a few additional tips for coping with triggers and

preventing relapses:

– Seek out professional help: If you are struggling to cope with triggers or prevent relapses, consider seeking the help of a trained therapist or coach. These professionals can provide a safe and supportive space to explore your feelings and develop coping strategies and patterns of behavior.

– Practice self-acceptance: Self-acceptance involves being accepting and non-judgmental towards yourself, including your flaws, mistakes, and limitations. It can be helpful in coping with triggers and preventing relapses, as it allows you to be more understanding and forgiving towards yourself and your limitations.

– Seek out new sources of support: In addition to your regular support network, there are many other resources available to help you cope with triggers and prevent relapses. These may include online support groups, helplines, and peer support programs. Consider seeking out new sources of support to help you navigate difficult times.

– Seek out healthy role models: Observing and learning from healthy relationships can be a helpful way to develop your own skills and patterns of behavior. Consider seeking out healthy role models, such as friends or family members who have strong and fulfilling relationships, and observing and learning from their communication and relationship patterns.

– Practice healthy self-care: Taking care of your own needs and well-being is an important aspect of coping with triggers and preventing relapses. This may involve setting aside time for yourself, engaging in activities that bring you joy and fulfillment, and seeking out the support you need when you are struggling.

It is also important to remember that it is normal to have setbacks and challenges in your journey towards recovery. If you do experience a relapse or struggle with triggers, it is important to be kind and understanding towards yourself and to remember that recovery is a journey that involves ups and downs.

Here are a few additional tips for coping with triggers and preventing relapses:

– Seek out support: If you are struggling to cope with triggers or prevent a relapse, it is important to seek out the support you need. This may involve reaching out to your support network, seeking the help of a therapist or coach, or joining a support group.

– Practice self-compassion: Self-compassion involves being kind and understanding towards yourself, especially during difficult times. It can be helpful in coping with triggers and preventing relapses, as it allows you to be more understanding and forgiving towards yourself and your limitations.

– Seek out healthy coping strategies: When faced with a trigger or at risk of a relapse, it is important to have a toolkit of healthy coping strategies to help you navigate the situation. These may include healthy self-care practices, such as exercise, meditation, or spending time in nature, or seeking the support of a trusted friend or therapist.

– Learn from your setbacks: If you do experience a relapse or struggle with triggers, try to view it as an opportunity to learn and grow. Reflect on what led to the setback, and consider what you can do differently in the future to prevent similar challenges.

– Seek out new opportunities for personal growth and development: Engaging in new experiences and challenges can help you to grow and develop new skills, which can in turn boost your self-worth and self-love. Consider seeking out new opportunities for personal growth and development, such as workshops, classes, or volunteer work.

By following these tips and seeking the right support, you can cope with triggers and prevent relapses in your journey towards recovery. Remember, dealing with triggers and preventing relapses is an ongoing process that requires patience, self-compassion, and a commitment to personal growth. It may take time and effort to make progress, and there may be setbacks along the way. However, with time, effort, and the right support, you can cope with triggers and prevent relapses and build a more fulfilling and healthy life for yourself.

12: Building a Fulfilling Life in Recovery

Building a fulfilling life in recovery can be a challenging but rewarding process. It involves exploring your values, goals, and interests, and taking steps to create a life that feels meaningful and fulfilling to you. Here are a few tips to help you build a fulfilling life in recovery:

– Explore your values and goals: Building a fulfilling life in recovery often involves identifying your values and goals, and taking steps to align your life with these values. This may involve exploring your interests and passions, and considering what brings you a sense of purpose and meaning.

– Seek out new opportunities for growth and development: Engaging in new experiences and challenges can help you to grow and develop new skills, which can in turn boost your self-worth and self-love. Consider seeking out new opportunities for personal growth and development, such as workshops, classes, or volunteer work.

– Build and maintain healthy relationships: Strong and supportive relationships are an important aspect of a fulfilling life. Consider building and maintaining healthy relationships with friends, family, and loved ones, and seeking out relationship education or therapy if needed.

– Practice self-care: Taking care of your own needs and well-being is an important aspect of building a fulfilling life in recovery. This may involve setting aside time for yourself, engaging in activities that bring you joy and fulfillment, and seeking out the support you need when you are struggling.

Find ways to contribute to your community: Building a fulfilling life often involves finding ways to give back and contribute to your community. Consider volunteering your time, skills, or resources to organizations or causes that are meaningful to you.

Here are a few more tips to help you build a fulfilling life in recovery:

– Practice gratitude: Practicing gratitude involves focusing on the positive aspects of your life, including your relationships. It can help to shift your perspective and to cultivate a sense of contentment and well-being. Consider starting a gratitude journal or sharing your gratitude with your partner on a regular basis.

– Seek out new sources of support: In addition to your regular support network, there are many other resources available to help you build a fulfilling life in recovery. These may include online support groups, helplines, and peer support programs. Consider seeking out new sources of support to help you navigate difficult times.

– Practice healthy communication: Effective communication is an important aspect of any healthy relationship. It involves being open and honest with your partner about your needs, boundaries, and feelings, and listening actively to your partner's perspective. Seek out resources, such as therapy or communication workshops, if you are struggling with communication in your relationship.

– Seek out new experiences and challenges: Engaging in new experiences and challenges can help you to grow and develop new skills, which can in turn boost your self-worth and self-love. Consider trying new hobbies or activities, or seeking out new opportunities for personal growth and development.

– Practice mindfulness: Mindfulness is the practice of being present in the moment, without judgment. It can be a helpful tool in building a fulfilling life in recovery, as it allows you to become more aware of your thoughts, feelings, and physical sensations, and to respond to them in a more healthy and balanced way.

Here are a few more tips to help you build a fulfilling life in recovery:

– Find healthy outlets for your emotions: It is normal to experience a range of emotions in recovery, including both positive and negative emotions. It is important to find healthy outlets for your emotions, such as through journaling, art, or exercise, rather than turning to unhealthy coping mechanisms like substance abuse or unhealthy relationships.

– Practice self-acceptance: Self-acceptance involves being accepting and non-judgmental towards yourself, including your flaws, mistakes, and limitations. It can be helpful in building a fulfilling life in recovery, as it allows you to be more understanding and forgiving towards yourself and your limitations.

– Seek out healthy role models: Observing and learning from healthy relationships can be a helpful way to develop your own skills and patterns of behavior. Consider seeking out healthy role models, such as friends or family members who have strong and fulfilling relationships, and observing and learning from their communication and relationship patterns.

– Learn from your setbacks: If you do experience setbacks or challenges in your journey towards recovery, try to view it as an opportunity to learn and grow. Reflect on what led to the setback, and consider what you can do differently in the future to prevent similar challenges.

– Practice forgiveness: Forgiveness involves letting go of resentment or anger towards others or yourself. It can be an important aspect of building a fulfilling life in recovery, as it allows you to move forward and to focus on your own growth and well-being. Consider seeking out resources, such as therapy or forgiveness workshops, to help you practice forgiveness.

– Practice gratitude: Practicing gratitude involves focusing on the positive aspects of your life, including your recovery journey. It can help to shift your perspective and to cultivate a sense of contentment and well-being. Consider starting a gratitude journal or sharing your gratitude with your support network on a regular basis.

– Find ways to contribute to your community: Building a fulfilling life often involves finding ways to give back and contribute to your community. Consider volunteering your time, skills, or resources to organizations or causes that are meaningful to you.

– Practice healthy self-care: Taking care of your own needs and well-being is an important aspect of building a fulfilling life in recovery. This may involve setting aside time for yourself, engaging in activities that bring you joy and fulfillment, and seeking out the support you need when you are struggling.

– Seek out new sources of support: In addition to your regular support network, there are many other resources available to help you build a fulfilling life in recovery. These may include online support groups, helplines, and peer support programs. Consider seeking out new sources of support to help you navigate difficult times.

– Practice mindfulness: Mindfulness is the practice of being present in the moment, without judgment. It can be a helpful tool in building a fulfilling life in recovery, as it allows you to become more aware of your thoughts, feelings, and physical sensations, and to respond to them in a more healthy and balanced way.

Practice forgiveness: Forgiveness involves letting go of resentment or anger towards others or yourself. It can be an important aspect of building a fulfilling life in recovery, as it allows you to move forward and to focus on your own growth and well-being. Consider seeking out resources, such as therapy or forgiveness workshops, to help you practice forgiveness.

– Learn from your setbacks: If you do experience setbacks or challenges in your journey towards recovery, try to view it as an opportunity to learn and grow. Reflect on what led to the setback, and consider what you can do differently in the future to prevent similar challenges.

– Seek out healthy role models: Observing and learning from healthy relationships can be a helpful way to develop your own skills and patterns of behavior. Consider seeking out healthy role models, such as friends or family members who have strong and fulfilling relationships, and observing and learning from their communication and relationship patterns.

– Practice self-acceptance: Self-acceptance involves being accepting and non-judgmental towards yourself, including your flaws, mistakes, and limitations. It can be helpful in building a fulfilling life in recovery, as it allows you to be more understanding and forgiving towards yourself and your limitations.

– Practice healthy self-care: Taking care of your own needs and well-being is an important aspect of building a fulfilling life in recovery. This may involve setting aside time for yourself, engaging in activities that bring you joy and fulfillment, and seeking out the support you need when you are struggling.

By following these tips and seeking the right support, you can build a fulfilling life in recovery. Remember, building a fulfilling life is an ongoing process that requires patience, self-compassion, and a commitment to personal growth. It may take time and effort to make progress, and there may be setbacks along the way. However, with time, effort, and the right support, you can build a fulfilling and healthy life for yourself.

13: Celebrating Your Journey of Healing and Self-discovery

Congratulations on making the brave and courageous decision to embark on a journey of healing and self-discovery! This is no small feat, and it is a testament to your strength and determination.

As you celebrate your progress, it is important to take the time to reflect on the journey you have been on. This may involve looking back on the challenges and struggles you have faced, as well as the moments of triumph and growth.

One way to celebrate your journey is to create a visual representation of your journey, such as a collage or a scrapbook. This can be a fun and creative way to reflect on your journey and to honor the progress you have made. You may also consider sharing your journey with others, such as through writing or art, or by speaking with a trusted friend or family member.

It is also important to celebrate your journey in more tangible ways. This may involve treating yourself to something special, such as a massage or a day out with friends. It is important to remember that you deserve to celebrate your progress and to take care of yourself.

As you celebrate your journey, it is also important to remember that recovery is an ongoing process. It is normal to have ups and downs, and it is important to be kind and understanding towards yourself when you experience setbacks. Remember, the journey of healing and self-discovery is one of growth and personal development, and it is a journey that you are undertaking for yourself.

As you continue on your journey, remember to be proud of the progress you have made, and to celebrate your journey of healing and self-discovery. You have come a long way, and you deserve to celebrate your journey and all that you have achieved. So, take the time to honor yourself and your journey, and remember to celebrate your progress along the way.

Here are a few more tips for celebrating your journey of healing and self-discovery:

– Practice gratitude: Practicing gratitude involves focusing on the positive aspects of your life, including your recovery journey. It can help to shift your perspective and to cultivate a sense of contentment and well-being. Consider starting a gratitude journal or sharing your gratitude with your support network on a regular basis.

– Seek out new experiences and challenges: Engaging in new experiences and challenges can help you to grow and develop new skills, which can in turn boost your self-worth and self-love. Consider trying new hobbies or activities, or seeking out new opportunities for personal growth and development.

– Seek out healthy role models: Observing and learning from healthy relationships can be a helpful way to develop your own skills and patterns of behavior. Consider seeking out healthy role models, such as friends or family members who have strong and fulfilling relationships, and observing and learning from their communication and relationship patterns.

– Practice healthy self-care: Taking care of your own needs and well-being is an important aspect of building a fulfilling life in recovery. This may involve setting aside time for yourself, engaging in activities that bring you joy and fulfillment, and seeking out the support you need when you are struggling.

– Find healthy outlets for your emotions: It is normal to experience a range of emotions in recovery, including both positive and negative emotions. It is important to find healthy outlets for your emotions, such as through journaling, art, or exercise, rather than turning to unhealthy coping mechanisms like substance abuse or unhealthy relationships.

– Practice self-compassion: Self-compassion involves being kind and understanding towards yourself, especially during difficult times. It can be helpful in building a fulfilling life in recovery, as it allows you to be more understanding and forgiving towards yourself and your limitations.

– Learn from your setbacks: If you do experience setbacks or challenges in your journey towards recovery, try to view it as an opportunity to learn and grow. Reflect on what led to the setback, and consider what you can do differently in the future to prevent similar challenges.

– Practice healthy communication: Effective communication is an important aspect of any healthy relationship. It

involves being open and honest with your partner about
your needs, boundaries, and feelings, and listening actively
to your partner's perspective. Seek out resources, such as
therapy or communication workshops, if you are struggling
with communication in your relationship.

– Build and maintain healthy relationships: Strong and
supportive relationships are an important aspect of a fulfilling life. Consider building and maintaining healthy relationships with friends, family, and loved ones, and seeking
out relationship education or therapy if needed.

– Practice forgiveness: Forgiveness involves letting go of resentment or anger towards others or yourself. It can be an
important aspect of building a fulfilling life in recovery, as it
allows you to move forward and to focus on your own
growth and well-being. Consider seeking out resources,
such as therapy or forgiveness workshops, to help you practice forgiveness.

– Seek out professional support: It can be helpful to seek
out professional support, such as therapy or coaching, to
help you navigate your journey of healing and self-discovery. A professional can provide you with guidance and sup-

port, and can help you to develop strategies and tools to manage challenges and setbacks.

– Set goals and celebrate your achievements: Setting goals and celebrating your achievements can help to keep you motivated and focused on your journey. Consider setting both short-term and long-term goals, and take the time to celebrate your progress along the way.

– Practice mindfulness: Mindfulness involves being present and aware in the moment, without judgment. It can be helpful in building a fulfilling life in recovery, as it allows you to be more present and engaged in your life and relationships. Consider seeking out resources, such as mindfulness meditation or yoga, to help you practice mindfulness.

– Seek out a supportive community: Building a supportive community of friends, family, and loved ones can be an important aspect of your journey of healing and self-discovery. Consider seeking out supportive communities, such as recovery groups or support groups, to help you connect with others who are on a similar journey.

– Take time for self-reflection: Self-reflection involves taking the time to reflect on your thoughts, feelings, and behaviors. It can be helpful in building a fulfilling life in recovery, as it allows you to gain insight into your own patterns and behaviors, and to make positive changes. Consider setting aside time each day or week for self-reflection, and consider seeking out resources, such as journaling or therapy, to help you practice self-reflection.

– Seek out healthy ways to manage stress: It is normal to experience stress as you navigate your journey of healing and self-discovery. However, it is important to find healthy ways to manage stress, such as through exercise, meditation, or hobbies, rather than turning to unhealthy coping mechanisms like substance abuse or unhealthy relationships.

– Practice self-acceptance: Self-acceptance involves being accepting and non-judgmental towards yourself, including your flaws, mistakes, and limitations. It can be helpful in building a fulfilling life in recovery, as it allows you to be more understanding and forgiving towards yourself and your limitations.

– Seek out new opportunities for personal growth: Personal

growth is an important aspect of building a fulfilling life in recovery. Consider seeking out new opportunities for personal growth, such as through education, hobbies, or volunteering.

– Practice gratitude: Practicing gratitude involves focusing on the positive aspects of your life, including your recovery journey. It can help to shift your perspective and to cultivate a sense of contentment and well-being. Consider starting a gratitude journal or sharing your gratitude with your support network on a regular basis.

– Seek out healthy role models: Observing and learning from healthy relationships can be a helpful way to develop your own skills and patterns of behavior. Consider seeking out healthy role models, such as friends or family members who have strong and fulfilling relationships, and observing and learning from their communication and relationship patterns.

As you continue on your journey of healing and self-discovery, remember to celebrate your progress and to take care of yourself. You have come a long way, and you deserve to celebrate your journey and all that you have achieved. So, take the time to honor yourself and your journey, and remember to celebrate your progress along the way.

Book 4 - Toxic Relationships

Navigating the Emotional Landmines of Toxic Relationships: A Survival Manual for Recognizing and Dealing with the Warning Signs of Dysfunctional Love, Gaslighting, and Emotional Abuse

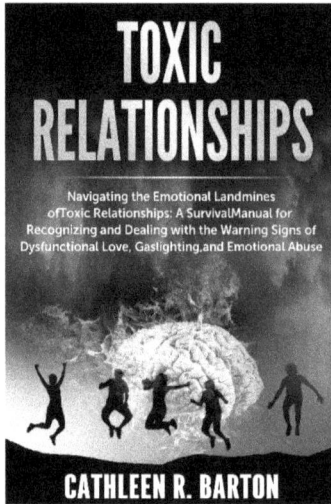

01: What is a Toxic Relationship?

A toxic relationship is one that is emotionally and/or physically damaging to one or both of the individuals involved. These types of relationships can be destructive and have a negative impact on the mental and emotional well-being of those involved.

There are many different forms that toxic relationships can take, but some common characteristics include:

– Control: One partner may try to control the other's behavior, decisions, or actions. This can include manipulating, threatening, or using intimidation tactics to get their way.

– Lack of respect: Disrespect can manifest in many ways in a toxic relationship, including verbal abuse, neglect, or even physical abuse.

– Lack of emotional support: A toxic partner may be emotionally distant or unavailable, leaving their partner feeling unsupported and alone.

– Unhealthy communication: Communication in a toxic relationship may be marked by criticism, blame, or stonewalling, rather than healthy, constructive communication.

01: WHAT IS A TOXIC RELATIONSHIP?

– Dishonesty: Lying, deceit, or hiding important information can be hallmarks of a toxic relationship.

– Insecurity: Insecurity in one or both partners may manifest as jealousy, possessiveness, or an inability to trust their partner.

Toxic relationships can occur in any type of relationship, including romantic relationships, friendships, and even familial relationships. They can be difficult to recognize, especially if you have been in the relationship for a long time and have become accustomed to the dynamic. It can be especially difficult to recognize if you have been conditioned to believe that the behavior is normal or acceptable.

It's important to recognize the signs of a toxic relationship and seek help if you are in one. This may include seeking therapy, reaching out to trusted friends or family members for support, or even leaving the relationship if it is safe to do so. It's also important to take care of yourself and prioritize your own well-being. This may include setting boundaries, practicing self-care, and building a support system outside of the toxic relationship.

It's never too late to make the decision to leave a toxic relationship and start on the path to healing. It can be a difficult and intimidating process, but it is worth it for your own happiness and well-being. Remember that you deserve to be in a healthy, supportive, and loving relationship.

It's important to note that toxic relationships are not always easy to recognize, especially if you have been in the relationship for a long time. You may have become accustomed to the dynamic and may not even realize that the way you are being treated is not healthy. It's also possible that your partner may try to convince you that their behavior is normal or that you are being too sensitive. This is known as gaslighting, and it is a common tactic used in toxic relationships to manipulate and control the other person.

It's essential to trust your instincts and pay attention to any red flags or warning signs that something may not be right in the relationship. Some common signs that you may be in a toxic relationship include:

– Feeling constantly criticized or belittled by your partner

– Feeling like you have to walk on eggshells around your partner to avoid their anger or criticism

01: WHAT IS A TOXIC RELATIONSHIP?

– Feeling like you are not good enough for your partner or that you have to constantly prove yourself

– Feeling like you are constantly being controlled or manipulated by your partner

– Feeling like you have lost your sense of self or your independence in the relationship

– Feeling like you are constantly being lied to or that your partner is not being honest with you

If you are experiencing any of these red flags, it's important to take them seriously and consider seeking help. A healthy relationship should be based on trust, respect, and mutual support, not control, manipulation, or abuse.

Leaving a toxic relationship can be a challenging and overwhelming process, but it is possible. It's important to make a plan and seek support from trusted friends, family members, or a therapist. It's also essential to have a safety plan in place if you are in a physically abusive relationship. This may include finding a safe place to go, having a support system in place, and knowing how to get help if you need it.

It's also crucial to take care of yourself and prioritize your own well-being during and after the process of leaving a toxic relationship. This may include setting boundaries, practicing self-care, and seeking therapy to help you process your experiences and heal.

Remember that you deserve to be in a healthy, supportive, and loving relationship. Don't let fear or insecurity hold you back from making the decision to leave a toxic relationship and start on the path to healing. You are not alone, and there is help and support available to you.

It's also important to remember that toxic relationships are not always easy to leave, especially if you have been in the relationship for a long time or if you have children together. You may feel afraid of what the future holds, or you may worry about how you will support yourself financially. These are valid concerns, but it's important to remember that you deserve to be in a healthy, supportive, and loving relationship.

There are resources available to help you navigate the process of leaving a toxic relationship. This may include reaching out to a trusted friend or family member for support, seeking therapy to help you process your experiences and heal, or reaching out to organizations that specialize in helping individuals leave abusive relationships.

It's also important to have a safety plan in place if you are in a physically abusive relationship. This may include finding a safe place to go, having a support system in place, and knowing how to get help if you need it.

Leaving a toxic relationship can be a challenging and overwhelming process, but it is possible. It's important to take things one step at a time and focus on taking care of yourself. This may include setting boundaries, practicing self-care, and seeking therapy to help you process your experiences and heal.

Remember that you are not alone, and there is help and support available to you. Don't let fear or insecurity hold you back from making the decision to leave a toxic relationship and start on the path to healing. You deserve to be in a healthy, supportive, and loving relationship, and you can get there with the right help and support.

02: The Warning Signs of a Dysfunctional Relationship

Dysfunctional relationships are characterized by unhealthy dynamics and patterns of behavior that can be emotionally and/or physically damaging to one or both individuals involved. These types of relationships can be challenging to recognize, especially if you have been in the relationship for a long time or if you have been conditioned to believe that the behavior is normal or acceptable.

It's important to be aware of the warning signs of a dysfunctional relationship and to seek help if you are in one. Some common signs to look out for include:

– Constant criticism or belittling: In a healthy relationship, both partners should feel supported and uplifted. If you are constantly being criticized or belittled by your partner, this is a red flag that something may not be right in the relationship.

– Lack of respect: Disrespect can manifest in many ways in a dysfunctional relationship, including verbal abuse, neglect, or even physical abuse. It's important to be with a partner who treats you with kindness and respect.

02: THE WARNING SIGNS OF A DYSFUNCTIONAL RE-LATIONSHIP

– Lack of emotional support: A dysfunctional partner may be emotionally distant or unavailable, leaving you feeling unsupported and alone. It's important to be with a partner who is there for you and who shows an interest in your well-being.

– Unhealthy communication: Communication in a dysfunctional relationship may be marked by criticism, blame, or stonewalling, rather than healthy, constructive communication. It's important to be with a partner who is willing to listen and communicate openly and honestly with you.

– Dishonesty: Lying, deceit, or hiding important information can be hallmarks of a dysfunctional relationship. It's essential to be with a partner who is honest and trustworthy.

– Insecurity: Insecurity in one or both partners may manifest as jealousy, possessiveness, or an inability to trust their partner. It's important to be with a partner who is confident and secure in themselves and in the relationship.

If you are experiencing any of these red flags, it's important to take them seriously and consider seeking help. A healthy relationship should be based on trust, respect, and mutual support, not control, manipulation, or abuse.

It's never too late to make the decision to leave a dysfunctional relationship and start on the path to healing. It can be a difficult and intimidating process, but it is worth it for your own happiness and well-being. Remember that you deserve to be in a healthy, supportive, and loving relationship.

It's also important to recognize that dysfunctional relationships can take many different forms and may not always be easy to recognize. You may have become accustomed to the dynamic and may not even realize that the way you are being treated is not healthy. It's also possible that your partner may try to convince you that their behavior is normal or that you are being too sensitive. This is known as gaslighting, and it is a common tactic used in dysfunctional relationships to manipulate and control the other person.

If you are unsure whether your relationship is healthy or not, it can be helpful to seek the advice of a trusted friend, family member, or therapist. They can provide an outside perspective and help you to see things more clearly.

It's also essential to take care of yourself and prioritize your own well-being if you are in a dysfunctional relationship. This may include setting boundaries, practicing self-care, and building a support system outside of the relationship. It's important to have a support system in place to help you through the process of leaving a dysfunctional relationship and to provide emotional and practical support during your recovery.

Leaving a dysfunctional relationship can be a challenging and overwhelming process, but it is possible. It's important to make a plan and seek support from trusted friends, family members, or a therapist. It's also essential to have a safety plan in place if you are in a physically abusive relationship. This may include finding a safe place to go, having a support system in place, and knowing how to get help if you need it.

It's also crucial to take care of yourself and prioritize your own well-being during and after the process of leaving a dysfunctional relationship. This may include setting boundaries, practicing self-care, and seeking therapy to help you process your experiences and heal.

02: THE WARNING SIGNS OF A DYSFUNCTIONAL RE-LATIONSHIP

Remember that you deserve to be in a healthy, supportive, and loving relationship. Don't let fear or insecurity hold you back from making the decision to leave a dysfunctional relationship and start on the path to healing. You are not alone, and there is help and support available to you.

It's important to remember that leaving a dysfunctional relationship can be a challenging and overwhelming process, especially if you have been in the relationship for a long time or if you have children together. You may feel afraid of what the future holds, or you may worry about how you will support yourself financially. These are valid concerns, but it's important to remember that you deserve to be in a healthy, supportive, and loving relationship.

There are resources available to help you navigate the process of leaving a dysfunctional relationship. This may include reaching out to a trusted friend or family member for support, seeking therapy to help you process your experiences and heal, or reaching out to organizations that specialize in helping individuals leave abusive relationships.

It's also essential to have a safety plan in place if you are in a physically abusive relationship. This may include finding a safe place to go, having a support system in place, and knowing how to get help if you need it.

Leaving a dysfunctional relationship can be a challenging and overwhelming process, but it is possible. It's important to take things one step at a time and focus on taking care of yourself. This may include setting boundaries, practicing self-care, and seeking therapy to help you process your experiences and heal.

Remember that you are not alone, and there is help and support available to you. Don't let fear or insecurity hold you back from making the decision to leave a dysfunctional relationship and start on the path to healing. You deserve to be in a healthy, supportive, and loving relationship, and you can get there with the right help and support.

03: Gaslighting: A Common Form of Emotional Abuse

Gaslighting is a form of emotional abuse in which the abuser manipulates the victim into doubting their own memories, perceptions, or judgment. This can be done through a variety of tactics, such as denying that certain events took place, manipulating evidence, or even planting false memories in the victim's mind.

The goal of gaslighting is to make the victim feel like they are going crazy and to undermine their sense of reality. It's a way for the abuser to exert control and manipulate the victim into doing what they want.

Gaslighting can be especially damaging because it can make the victim feel like they are losing their grip on reality. They may start to question their own memories, perceptions, and judgment, which can lead to feelings of confusion, anxiety, and even depression.

Some common signs that you may be a victim of gaslighting include:

— Being told that you are imagining things or that certain

events never happened

– Being made to feel like you are being unreasonable or overly sensitive

– Being told that you are misremembering things or that your memories are flawed

– Feeling like you are constantly second-guessing yourself or questioning your own judgment

– Feeling like you are going crazy or that something is wrong with you

It's important to recognize the signs of gaslighting and to seek help if you are a victim. Gaslighting is a form of emotional abuse, and it is not acceptable behavior. It's essential to be with a partner who treats you with kindness, respect, and honesty.

If you are a victim of gaslighting, it's important to seek support from trusted friends, family members, or a therapist. They can provide an outside perspective and help you to see things more clearly. It's also essential to practice self-care and to prioritize your own well-being. This may include setting boundaries, seeking therapy, and building a support system outside of the abusive relationship.

Leaving an abusive relationship is a challenging and overwhelming process, but it is possible. It's important to make a plan and to seek the help and support that you need. Remember that you deserve to be in a healthy, supportive, and loving relationship, and you can get there with the right help and support.

It's important to remember that gaslighting is a form of emotional abuse, and it is not your fault if you are a victim. The abuser is responsible for their behavior, and it is not up to you to fix them or to make them change.

If you are in a relationship where you are being gaslighted, it's essential to prioritize your own well-being and to seek the help and support that you need. This may include seeking therapy, reaching out to trusted friends or family members for support, or even leaving the relationship if it is safe to do so.

Leaving an abusive relationship can be a challenging and overwhelming process, but it is possible. It's important to make a plan and to seek the help and support that you need. This may include finding a safe place to go, having a support system in place, and knowing how to get help if you need it.

It's also crucial to take care of yourself and to practice self-care during and after the process of leaving an abusive relationship. This may include setting boundaries, seeking therapy, and building a support system outside of the abusive relationship.

Remember that you deserve to be in a healthy, supportive, and loving relationship, and you can get there with the right help and support. Don't let fear or insecurity hold you back from making the decision to leave an abusive relationship and start on the path to healing. You are not alone, and there is help and support available to you.

It's essential to remember that healing from an abusive relationship, including one where you have been gaslighted, takes time. It's important to be patient with yourself and to allow yourself the time and space to process your experiences and heal.

Seeking therapy can be an important part of the healing process. A therapist can provide a safe and supportive space for you to talk about your experiences and to work through your feelings. They can also help you to develop healthy coping strategies and to set boundaries to protect yourself in the future.

It's also crucial to build a support system outside of the abusive relationship. This may include reaching out to trusted friends and family members, joining a support group, or seeking the help of a counselor or therapist. It's important to have people in your life who can provide emotional and practical support as you navigate the process of healing and moving forward.

It's also essential to practice self-care and to prioritize your own well-being. This may include setting boundaries, engaging in activities that bring you joy, and taking time for yourself to rest and recharge. It's important to remember that you deserve to be treated with kindness, respect, and love, and to surround yourself with people who reflect those values.

Leaving an abusive relationship is a challenging and overwhelming process, but it is possible. It's important to re-member that you deserve to be in a healthy, supportive, and loving relationship, and it's okay to take the time you need to heal and to focus on your own well-being. It's important to be patient with yourself and to give yourself grace as you navigate this process.

It's also crucial to remember that healing is not a linear pro-cess, and you may experience setbacks or moments of struggle along the way. This is normal, and it's important to be kind to yourself and to seek support when you need it.

As you begin to heal and move forward, it's essential to be mindful of the lessons you have learned from your past ex-periences. This may include learning how to set boundaries, how to recognize the warning signs of an unhealthy rela-tionship, and how to advocate for your own needs and well-being.

It's also important to remember that you are not alone, and there is help and support available to you. Don't be afraid to reach out for help if you need it, and remember that you de-serve to be in a healthy, supportive, and loving relationship. You have the strength and resilience to overcome your past experiences and to create a bright and fulfilling future for yourself.

04: The Impact of Toxic Relationships on Mental Health

Toxic relationships can have a significant impact on an individual's mental health. The constant negativity, criticism, manipulation, and emotional abuse can take a toll on a person's self-esteem, confidence, and overall well-being.

One of the most common mental health impacts of toxic relationships is depression. The constant negativity and criticism can lead to feelings of worthlessness and hopelessness, which can manifest as depression. The emotional abuse can also lead to feelings of isolation and loneliness, which can further contribute to depression.

Anxiety is another common mental health impact of toxic relationships. The constant stress and uncertainty of being in a toxic relationship can lead to feelings of anxiety and worry. The fear of being criticized or punished can also lead to feelings of anxiety.

Toxic relationships can also lead to low self-esteem and a lack of confidence. The constant belittling and criticism can erode an individual's sense of self-worth, leading to low self-esteem. The manipulation and control tactics used in toxic relationships can also make it difficult for individuals to trust their own judgment and to feel confident in their decisions.

Toxic relationships can also lead to post-traumatic stress disorder (PTSD). The emotional and psychological abuse can be traumatic and may lead to symptoms of PTSD, such as flashbacks, nightmares, and avoidance of triggers.

It's important to recognize the impact that toxic relationships can have on mental health and to seek help if you are in a toxic relationship. A therapist or counselor can help you to work through the mental health impacts of the toxic relationship and to develop healthy coping strategies. It's also essential to prioritize your own well-being and to take care of yourself during and after the process of leaving a toxic relationship. This may include setting boundaries, practicing self-care, and seeking therapy to help you process your experiences and heal.

Remember that you deserve to be in a healthy, supportive, and loving relationship, and it's never too late to make the decision to leave a toxic relationship and start on the path to healing. You are not alone, and there is help and support available to you.

It's also important to remember that healing from the mental health impacts of a toxic relationship takes time. It's important to be patient with yourself and to allow yourself the time and space to process your experiences and heal.

Seeking therapy can be an important part of the healing process. A therapist can provide a safe and supportive space for you to talk about your experiences and to work through your feelings. They can also help you to develop healthy coping strategies and to set boundaries to protect yourself in the future.

It's also crucial to build a support system outside of the toxic relationship. This may include reaching out to trusted friends and family members, joining a support group, or seeking the help of a counselor or therapist. It's important to have people in your life who can provide emotional and practical support as you navigate the process of healing and moving forward.

It's also essential to practice self-care and to prioritize your own well-being. This may include setting boundaries, engaging in activities that bring you joy, and taking time for yourself to rest and recharge. It's important to remember that you deserve to be treated with kindness, respect, and love, and to surround yourself with people who reflect those values.

Leaving a toxic relationship is a challenging and overwhelming process, but it is possible. It's important to remember that you deserve to be in a healthy, supportive, and loving relationship, and it's okay to take the time you need to heal and to focus on your own well-being. It's important to be patient with yourself and to give yourself grace as you navigate this process.

As you begin to heal and move forward, it's essential to be mindful of the lessons you have learned from your past experiences. This may include learning how to set boundaries, how to recognize the warning signs of an unhealthy relationship, and how to advocate for your own needs and well-being.

It's also important to remember that healing is not a linear process, and you may experience setbacks or moments of struggle along the way. This is normal, and it's important to be kind to yourself and to seek support when you need it.

One thing that can be helpful in the healing process is find-ing ways to practice self-care and to prioritize your own well-being. This may include setting boundaries, engaging in activities that bring you joy, and taking time for yourself to rest and recharge. It's important to remember that you deserve to be treated with kindness, respect, and love, and to surround yourself with people who reflect those values.

It's also essential to seek support and to build a strong sup-port system outside of the toxic relationship. This may in-clude reaching out to trusted friends and family members, joining a support group, or seeking the help of a counselor or therapist. It's important to have people in your life who can provide emotional and practical support as you navigate the process of healing and moving forward.

Remember that you are not alone, and there is help and support available to you. Don't be afraid to reach out for help if you need it, and remember that you deserve to be in a healthy, supportive, and loving relationship. You have the strength and resilience to overcome your past experiences and to create a bright and fulfilling future for yourself.

05: Recognizing the Patterns of Emotional Abuse

Emotional abuse is a pattern of behavior that is used to manipulate, control, and belittle another person. It can be difficult to recognize emotional abuse, especially if you have been in the relationship for a long time or if the abuse is subtle.

One way to recognize the patterns of emotional abuse is to pay attention to how you feel in the relationship. If you feel constantly criticized, belittled, or blamed, these are red flags of emotional abuse. If you feel like you are walking on eggshells around your partner or that you are constantly trying to please them, these are also signs of emotional abuse.

Another pattern of emotional abuse is gaslighting, which is when the abuser manipulates the victim into doubting their own memories, perceptions, or judgment. If you feel like you are constantly second-guessing yourself or that your partner is trying to make you feel like you are going crazy, these are signs of gaslighting.

It's also important to pay attention to the dynamics of the relationship. In an emotionally abusive relationship, the ab-

user may try to control every aspect of the victim's life, including their decisions, their relationships, and even their
thoughts and feelings. If you feel like your partner is constantly trying to control you or that you have lost your sense
of independence in the relationship, these are signs of emotional abuse.

It's important to recognize the patterns of emotional abuse
and to seek help if you are in an emotionally abusive relationship. Emotional abuse is not acceptable behavior, and
you deserve to be in a healthy, supportive, and loving relationship.

If you are in an emotionally abusive relationship, it's important to seek support from trusted friends, family members, or a therapist. They can provide an outside perspective
and help you to see things more clearly. It's also essential to
practice self-care and to prioritize your own well-being. This
may include setting boundaries, seeking therapy, and building a support system outside of the abusive relationship.

Leaving an emotionally abusive relationship is a challenging
and overwhelming process, but it is possible. It's important
to make a plan and to seek the help and support that you

need. Remember that you deserve to be in a healthy, supportive, and loving relationship, and you can get there with
the right help and support.

It's essential to remember that healing from an emotionally
abusive relationship takes time. It's important to be patient
with yourself and to allow yourself the time and space to
process your experiences and heal.

Seeking therapy can be an important part of the healing
process. A therapist can provide a safe and supportive space
for you to talk about your experiences and to work through
your feelings. They can also help you to develop healthy
coping strategies and to set boundaries to protect yourself
in the future.

It's also crucial to build a support system outside of the
emotionally abusive relationship. This may include reaching
out to trusted friends and family members, joining a support group, or seeking the help of a counselor or therapist.
It's important to have people in your life who can provide
emotional and practical support as you navigate the process
of healing and moving forward.

It's also essential to practice self-care and to prioritize your own well-being. This may include setting boundaries, engaging in activities that bring you joy, and taking time for yourself to rest and recharge. It's important to remember that you deserve to be treated with kindness, respect, and love, and to surround yourself with people who reflect those values.

Leaving an emotionally abusive relationship is a challenging and overwhelming process, but it is possible. It's important to remember that you deserve to be in a healthy, supportive, and loving relationship, and it's okay to take the time you need to heal and to focus on your own well-being. It's important to be patient with yourself and to give yourself grace as you navigate this process.

As you begin to heal and move forward, it's essential to be mindful of the lessons you have learned from your past experiences. This may include learning how to set boundaries, how to recognize the warning signs of an unhealthy relationship, and how to advocate for your own needs and well-being.

It's also important to remember that healing is not a linear process, and you may experience setbacks or moments of struggle along the way. This is normal, and it's important to be kind to yourself and to seek support when you need it.

Remember that you are not alone, and there is help and support available to you. Don't be afraid to reach out for help if you need it, and remember that you deserve to be in a healthy, supportive, and loving relationship. You have the strength and resilience to overcome your past experiences and to create a bright and fulfilling future for yourself.

Another way to recognize the patterns of emotional abuse is to pay attention to the language and communication patterns in the relationship. Emotional abusers often use language as a way to control and manipulate their victims. This may include using words to demean, belittle, or blame the victim, or using passive-aggressive or manipulative language to get what they want.

It's also common for emotional abusers to use threats or intimidation as a way to control their victims. This may include threats of violence, threats to harm themselves or others, or threats to end the relationship.

05: RECOGNIZING THE PATTERNS OF EMOTIONAL ABUSE

It's important to be aware of these patterns of communication and to recognize them as red flags of emotional abuse. If you feel like your partner is constantly using language or communication to control or manipulate you, it's essential to seek help and to prioritize your own well-being.

Another pattern of emotional abuse is isolating the victim from their friends, family, and other support systems. Emotional abusers may try to keep their victims isolated and away from others as a way to maintain control and to make it more difficult for the victim to seek help.

If you feel like your partner is trying to isolate you or keep you away from your support systems, it's important to recognize this as a red flag of emotional abuse. It's essential to maintain connections with trusted friends and family members and to seek help and support if you are in an emotionally abusive relationship.

Recognizing the patterns of emotional abuse is an important step in seeking help and in finding a way out of the toxic relationship. It's essential to prioritize your own well-being and to seek the help and support that you need to heal and move forward. You deserve to be in a healthy, supportive,

and loving relationship, and there is help and support available to you.

06: The Cycle of Toxic Relationships

Toxic relationships often follow a predictable pattern, known as the cycle of abuse. This cycle can be divided into four stages: the honeymoon stage, the tension-building stage, the explosion stage, and the honeymoon stage.

The honeymoon stage is characterized by feelings of love and affection. The abuser may be charming and loving, and the relationship may feel intense and passionate. This stage is often referred to as the "honeymoon" stage because it feels like the beginning of a new and exciting relationship.

The tension-building stage is characterized by an increase in tension and conflict. The abuser may start to display controlling or abusive behavior, and the victim may start to feel anxious or on edge. This stage can last for a long time, and the victim may start to feel like they are walking on eggshells to avoid triggering the abuser's anger.

The explosion stage is characterized by a sudden and explosive outburst of anger or violence. The abuser may lash out with physical, verbal, or emotional abuse, and the victim may feel scared or threatened. This stage is often followed by a sense of remorse or apology from the abuser, who may promise to change or to never behave that way again.

The honeymoon stage is characterized by a return to the feelings of love and affection from the beginning of the cycle. The abuser may be charming and loving again, and the victim may feel hopeful that the abuser has changed. This stage is often referred to as the "honeymoon" stage because it feels like the beginning of a new and exciting relationship.

This cycle can repeat itself over and over, with the victim feeling caught in a never-ending cycle of abuse and manipulation. It's important to recognize the cycle of abuse and to seek help if you are in a toxic relationship.

It's essential to remember that you deserve to be in a healthy, supportive, and loving relationship, and it's never too late to make the decision to leave a toxic relationship and start on the path to healing. You are not alone, and there is help and support available to you.

Leaving a toxic relationship can be a challenging and overwhelming process, but it is possible. It's important to make a plan and to seek the help and support that you need. This may include seeking therapy, building a support system, and setting boundaries to protect yourself.

It's also essential to practice self-care and to prioritize your own well-being. This may include engaging in activities that bring you joy, taking time for yourself to rest and recharge, and setting boundaries to protect yourself.

It's important to remember that healing from a toxic relationship takes time. It's essential to be patient with yourself and to allow yourself the time and space to process your experiences and heal.

Seeking therapy can be an important part of the healing process. A therapist can provide a safe and supportive space for you to talk about your experiences and to work through your feelings. They can also help you to develop healthy coping strategies and to set boundaries to protect yourself in the future.

It's also crucial to build a support system outside of the toxic relationship. This may include reaching out to trusted friends and family members, joining a support group, or seeking the help of a counselor or therapist. It's important to have people in your life who can provide emotional and practical support as you navigate the process of healing and moving forward.

Remember that you are not alone, and there is help and support available to you. Don't be afraid to reach out for help if you need it, and remember that you deserve to be in a healthy, supportive, and loving relationship. It's important to be patient with yourself and to give yourself grace as you navigate the process of healing and moving forward.

As you begin to heal and move forward, it's essential to be mindful of the lessons you have learned from your past experiences. This may include learning how to set boundaries, how to recognize the warning signs of an unhealthy relationship, and how to advocate for your own needs and well-being.

It's also important to remember that healing is not a linear process, and you may experience setbacks or moments of struggle along the way. This is normal, and it's important to be kind to yourself and to seek support when you need it.

One thing that can be helpful in the healing process is finding ways to practice self-care and to prioritize your own well-being. This may include setting boundaries, engaging in activities that bring you joy, and taking time for yourself to rest and recharge. It's important to remember that you deserve to be treated with kindness, respect, and love, and to surround yourself with people who reflect those values.

It's also essential to seek support and to build a strong support system outside of the toxic relationship. This may include reaching out to trusted friends and family members, joining a support group, or seeking the help of a counselor or therapist. It's important to have people in your life who can provide emotional and practical support as you navigate the process of healing and moving forward.

Remember that you are not alone, and there is help and support available to you. Don't be afraid to reach out for help if you need it, and remember that you deserve to be in a healthy, supportive, and loving relationship. You have the strength and resilience to overcome your past experiences and to create a bright and fulfilling future for yourself.

07: Breaking the Cycle: Making the Decision to Leave

Making the decision to leave a toxic relationship is a brave and difficult decision, but it can also be the first step towards healing and finding a healthy, supportive, and loving relationship.

It's important to remember that leaving a toxic relationship is not a sign of weakness, but rather a sign of strength and resilience. It takes courage to recognize that you deserve to be in a healthy and supportive relationship, and to take the steps necessary to make that happen.

Before making the decision to leave, it's important to consider your safety and to make a plan. This may include seeking support from trusted friends and family members, reaching out to a domestic violence hotline or shelter, and making a plan for where you will go and how you will support yourself.

It's also essential to remember that leaving a toxic relationship is a process, and it may not happen all at once. You may need to leave and return multiple times before you are ready to fully end the relationship. It's important to be patient with yourself and to give yourself grace as you navigate this process.

It's also crucial to seek support and to build a strong support system outside of the toxic relationship. This may include reaching out to trusted friends and family members, joining a support group, or seeking the help of a therapist or counselor. It's important to have people in your life who can provide emotional and practical support as you navigate the process of healing and moving forward.

It's also essential to practice self-care and to prioritize your own well-being. This may include setting boundaries, engaging in activities that bring you joy, and taking time for yourself to rest and recharge. It's important to remember that you deserve to be treated with kindness, respect, and love, and to surround yourself with people who reflect those values.

Remember that you are not alone, and there is help and support available to you. Don't be afraid to reach out for help if you need it, and remember that you deserve to be in a healthy, supportive, and loving relationship. You have the strength and resilience to overcome your past experiences and to create a bright and fulfilling future for yourself.

As you navigate the process of leaving a toxic relationship, it's important to be patient with yourself and to give yourself grace. Healing from a toxic relationship takes time, and it's important to allow yourself the time and space you need to process your experiences and heal.

It's also essential to seek support and to build a strong support system outside of the toxic relationship. This may include reaching out to trusted friends and family members, joining a support group, or seeking the help of a therapist or counselor. It's important to have people in your life who can provide emotional and practical support as you navigate the process of healing and moving forward.

It's also crucial to practice self-care and to prioritize your own well-being. This may include setting boundaries, engaging in activities that bring you joy, and taking time for yourself to rest and recharge. It's important to remember that you deserve to be treated with kindness, respect, and love, and to surround yourself with people who reflect those values.

07: BREAKING THE CYCLE: MAKING THE DECISION TO LEAVE

As you begin to heal and move forward, it's essential to be mindful of the lessons you have learned from your past experiences. This may include learning how to set boundaries, how to recognize the warning signs of an unhealthy relationship, and how to advocate for your own needs and well-being.

It's also important to remember that healing is not a linear process, and you may experience setbacks or moments of struggle along the way. This is normal, and it's important to be kind to yourself and to seek support when you need it.

Remember that you are not alone, and there is help and support available to you. Don't be afraid to reach out for help if you need it, and remember that you deserve to be in a healthy, supportive, and loving relationship. You have the strength and resilience to overcome your past experiences and to create a bright and fulfilling future for yourself.

As you continue to heal and move forward after leaving a toxic relationship, it's important to focus on your own well-being and to prioritize self-care. This may include setting boundaries, engaging in activities that bring you joy, and taking time for yourself to rest and recharge. It's essential to remember that you deserve to be treated with kindness, respect, and love, and to surround yourself with people who reflect those values.

It's also important to continue to seek support and to build a strong support system outside of the toxic relationship. This may include reaching out to trusted friends and family members, joining a support group, or seeking the help of a therapist or counselor. It's essential to have people in your life who can provide emotional and practical support as you navigate the process of healing and moving forward.

As you continue to heal and move forward, it's also important to be mindful of the lessons you have learned from your past experiences. This may include learning how to set boundaries, how to recognize the warning signs of an unhealthy relationship, and how to advocate for your own needs and well-being.

It's also essential to remember that healing is not a linear process, and you may experience setbacks or moments of struggle along the way. This is normal, and it's important to be kind to yourself and to seek support when you need it.

It's also important to remember that you are not alone, and there is help and support available to you. Don't be afraid to reach out for help if you need it, and remember that you deserve to be in a healthy, supportive, and loving relationship. You have the strength and resilience to overcome your past experiences and to create a bright and fulfilling future for yourself.

08: The Process of Healing After a Toxic Relationship

Healing after a toxic relationship is a process that takes time, patience, and self-care. It's important to remember that you are not alone, and there is help and support available to you. Here are a few tips to help you navigate the process of healing after a toxic relationship:

– Seek support: It's essential to build a strong support system outside of the toxic relationship. This may include reaching out to trusted friends and family members, joining a support group, or seeking the help of a therapist or counselor. It's important to have people in your life who can provide emotional and practical support as you navigate the process of healing and moving forward.

– Practice self-care: It's crucial to prioritize your own well-being and to practice self-care. This may include setting boundaries, engaging in activities that bring you joy, and taking time for yourself to rest and recharge. It's essential to remember that you deserve to be treated with kindness, respect, and love, and to surround yourself with people who reflect those values.

08: THE PROCESS OF HEALING AFTER A TOXIC RELATIONSHIP

– Be patient: Healing after a toxic relationship takes time, and it's important to be patient with yourself and to give yourself grace. It's normal to experience setbacks or moments of struggle along the way, and it's essential to be kind to yourself and to seek support when you need it.

– Learn from your experiences: As you continue to heal and move forward, it's important to be mindful of the lessons you have learned from your past experiences. This may include learning how to set boundaries, how to recognize the warning signs of an unhealthy relationship, and how to advocate for your own needs and well-being.

– Remember that you are not alone: It's essential to remember that you are not alone, and there is help and support available to you. Don't be afraid to reach out for help if you need it, and remember that you deserve to be in a healthy, supportive, and loving relationship. You have the strength and resilience to overcome your past experiences and to create a bright and fulfilling future for yourself.

Here are a few additional tips to help you navigate the process of healing after a toxic relationship:

08: THE PROCESS OF HEALING AFTER A TOXIC RELATIONSHIP

– Seek therapy: Therapy can be a helpful tool in the healing process, as it provides a safe and supportive space to talk about your experiences and to work through your feelings. A therapist can also help you to develop healthy coping strategies and to set boundaries to protect yourself in the future.

– Take time for yourself: It's important to allow yourself the time and space you need to heal. This may include taking breaks from social media, setting aside time for self-care, and finding activities that bring you joy and relaxation.

– Be kind to yourself: It's essential to be kind to yourself and to remember that you are not to blame for the toxic behavior of your partner. It's important to be gentle with yourself and to give yourself grace as you navigate the process of healing and moving forward.

– Set boundaries: Setting boundaries is an important part of the healing process, as it helps to protect you and to ensure that you are taking care of yourself. This may include setting limits on communication with your ex-partner, setting boundaries with friends and family members who may not fully understand your experiences, and saying no to situations that are not healthy or supportive.

– Remember that you deserve love and support: It's essential to remember that you deserve to be in a healthy, supportive, and loving relationship. Don't settle for less than you deserve, and remember that you have the strength and resilience to create a bright and fulfilling future for yourself.

Here are a few additional tips to help you navigate the process of healing after a toxic relationship:

– Find healthy ways to cope: It's important to find healthy ways to cope with your feelings and to manage stress. This may include engaging in activities like exercise, journaling, or spending time in nature.

– Seek out healthy relationships: Surrounding yourself with healthy and supportive relationships can be an important part of the healing process. Seek out friendships and relationships with people who are kind, respectful, and supportive.

– Learn to trust yourself: Trusting yourself and your own judgment is an important part of the healing process. Remember that you have the strength and resilience to make healthy decisions for yourself, and don't be afraid to trust your own instincts.

– Seek closure: Finding closure after a toxic relationship can be a helpful part of the healing process. This may involve having a conversation with your ex-partner to discuss your experiences and to find resolution, or it may involve finding closure in other ways, such as through therapy or by writing about your experiences.

– Remember that you are not alone: It's important to remember that you are not alone, and that there is help and support available to you. Don't be afraid to reach out for help if you need it, and remember that you deserve to be in a healthy, supportive, and loving relationship. You have the strength and resilience to overcome your past experiences and to create a bright and fulfilling future for yourself.

09: Setting Boundaries in Future Relationships

Setting boundaries is an essential part of any healthy relationship, and it's especially important after experiencing a toxic relationship. Boundaries are the limits we set with others to protect ourselves and to ensure that our needs and well-being are being respected. Setting boundaries can help to prevent us from being taken advantage of or mistreated, and it can also help to create a sense of respect and trust in our relationships.

Here are a few tips for setting boundaries in future relationships:

– Know your own needs and values: It's essential to be clear about your own needs and values, as this will help you to set boundaries that are in alignment with who you are and what you need. Take some time to reflect on what is most important to you and what you need in a relationship to feel safe, respected, and supported.

– Communicate your boundaries clearly: Once you know your own needs and values, it's important to communicate your boundaries clearly and assertively. This may involve saying things like "I don't feel comfortable with that," or "I need some space." It's essential to be clear and direct in your communication, and to not be afraid to advocate for your own needs.

− Respect the boundaries of others: It's important to respect the boundaries of others, even if they are different from your own. This may involve compromising or finding ways to negotiate your needs and boundaries with your partner. Remember that respecting the boundaries of others is an essential part of creating a healthy and respectful relationship.

− Be willing to compromise: In any relationship, there will be times when you may need to compromise or negotiate your boundaries. It's important to be open to this process and to be willing to find solutions that work for both parties.

− Seek support: If you are having difficulty setting boundaries or advocating for your own needs, it can be helpful to seek the support of a therapist or counselor. They can provide a safe and supportive space to work through any challenges you may be facing and to develop healthy coping strategies.

09: SETTING BOUNDARIES IN FUTURE RELATION- SHIPS

Remember that setting boundaries is an ongoing process, and it's important to continue to communicate and advocate for your own needs in your relationships. Don't be afraid to set boundaries and to assertively communicate your needs, and remember that you deserve to be in a healthy, respectful, and supportive relationship.

Here are a few additional tips for setting boundaries in future relationships:

– Don't be afraid to say no: It's important to remember that it's okay to say no and to set boundaries, even if it means disappointing someone else. Saying no is an essential part of taking care of yourself and ensuring that your own needs and well-being are being respected.

– Be consistent: It's important to be consistent in your communication and in enforcing your boundaries. This will help to create a sense of respect and trust in your relationships.

– Don't be afraid to seek help: If you are struggling to set boundaries or if you are in a relationship that is not healthy or respectful, it's important to seek help. This may include reaching out to a therapist or counselor, or seeking the support of trusted friends and family members.

– Remember that it's okay to end a relationship: If you are in a relationship that is not healthy or respectful, it's important to remember that it's okay to end the relationship. It's better to be alone than to be in a relationship that is toxic or abusive.

– Don't be afraid to seek help: If you are struggling to set boundaries or if you are in a relationship that is not healthy or respectful, it's important to seek help. This may include reaching out to a therapist or counselor, or seeking the support of trusted friends and family members. Remember that you deserve to be in a healthy, respectful, and supportive relationship, and that there is help and support available to you.

Here are a few additional tips for setting boundaries in future relationships:

– Practice self-care: Taking care of yourself is an essential part of setting boundaries and maintaining a healthy relationship. Make sure to set aside time for self-care, and prioritize activities that bring you joy and relaxation.

09: SETTING BOUNDARIES IN FUTURE RELATION-SHIPS

– Seek out supportive relationships: Surrounding yourself with healthy and supportive relationships can be an important part of setting boundaries and maintaining a healthy relationship. Seek out friendships and relationships with people who are kind, respectful, and supportive.

– Set boundaries with friends and family: It's not just romantic relationships that require boundaries. It's also important to set boundaries with friends and family members to ensure that your needs and well-being are being respected.

– Remember that it's okay to change your boundaries: As you grow and change, your boundaries may also change. It's important to be open to this process and to be willing to communicate and negotiate your boundaries with your partner.

– Seek therapy: If you are struggling to set boundaries or if you are in a relationship that is not healthy or respectful, it may be helpful to seek the support of a therapist or counselor. They can provide a safe and supportive space to work through any challenges you may be facing and to develop healthy coping strategies.

10: Communication Strategies for Dealing with a Toxic Partner

Effective communication is an essential part of any healthy relationship, and it's especially important when dealing with a toxic partner. Communication is the key to setting boundaries, advocating for your own needs, and finding resolution in conflicts. However, it can be challenging to communicate effectively with a toxic partner, as they may be resistant to change or unwilling to listen to your perspective. Here are a few communication strategies to consider when dealing with a toxic partner:

– Use "I" statements: "I" statements are a helpful tool for expressing your own thoughts and feelings without attacking the other person. For example, you could say "I feel hurt when you speak to me disrespectfully," rather than "You are always disrespectful to me." "I" statements can help to de-escalate conflicts and to keep the focus on your own feelings and experiences.

– Practice active listening: Active listening is a communication technique that involves fully paying attention to the other person, asking clarifying questions, and reflecting back what you have heard. This can help to create a sense of understanding and respect, and it can also help to reduce misunderstandings.

– Set boundaries: Setting boundaries is an essential part of effective communication, as it helps to protect you and to ensure that your needs and well-being are being respected. It's important to be clear and direct in communicating your boundaries, and to be assertive in enforcing them.

– Seek outside support: If you are struggling to communicate effectively with your toxic partner, it may be helpful to seek the support of a therapist or counselor. They can provide a safe and supportive space to work through any challenges you may be facing and to develop healthy communication strategies.

– Remember that you have the right to be heard: It's important to remember that you have the right to be heard and to have your feelings and needs respected. Don't be afraid to advocate for yourself and to communicate your needs, even if it is difficult or uncomfortable.

Communication is an ongoing process, and it's important to be patient and to continue to work on your communication skills, even if it is challenging. Remember that you deserve to be in a healthy, respectful, and supportive relationship, and that there is help and support available to you.

Here are a few additional communication strategies for dealing with a toxic partner:

— Take breaks: If you are in the midst of a heated argument, it may be helpful to take a break to cool down and to give yourself time to process your thoughts and feelings. It's important to remember that it's okay to take a break and to set boundaries to protect yourself.

— Use "we" statements: "We" statements can be a helpful tool for expressing a shared problem or concern, and for finding solutions together. For example, you could say "We seem to be having trouble communicating effectively, can we talk about how we can improve this?" "We" statements can help to shift the focus from blame to finding solutions together.

— Avoid toxic communication patterns: Toxic communication patterns, such as criticism, stonewalling, or contempt, can be damaging to a relationship and can escalate conflicts.

10: COMMUNICATION STRATEGIES FOR DEALING WITH A TOXIC PARTNER

It's important to be aware of these patterns and to work on finding healthier ways to communicate.

– Seek help: If you are struggling to communicate effectively with your toxic partner, or if you are in a relationship that is not healthy or respectful, it's important to seek help. This may include reaching out to a therapist or counselor, or seeking the support of trusted friends and family members.

– Remember that you deserve respect: It's essential to remember that you deserve to be treated with respect and kindness, and to advocate for yourself if your needs and boundaries are not being respected. Don't be afraid to communicate your needs, and remember that you have the right to be in a healthy, respectful, and supportive relationship.

Here are a few additional communication strategies for dealing with a toxic partner:

– Find common ground: It can be helpful to try to find common ground or shared interests as a way to build a sense of connection and understanding. This may involve finding activities you both enjoy or finding ways to support each other's passions and interests.

– Practice forgiveness: Forgiveness is not about condoning harmful behavior, but rather about letting go of resentment and anger. It can be a difficult process, but it can also be an important step towards healing and moving forward in a healthy way.

– Be open to change: Change can be difficult, but it's important to be open to the possibility of change in yourself and in your partner. This may involve seeking therapy or other forms of support, or simply being open to new ways of thinking and behaving.

– Practice gratitude: Focusing on gratitude and the positive aspects of your relationship can be a helpful way to shift your perspective and to build a sense of connection.

– Remember that you are not alone: It's important to remember that you are not alone, and that there is help and support available to you. Don't be afraid to reach out for help if you need it, and remember that you deserve to be in a healthy, respectful, and supportive relationship. You have the strength and resilience to overcome any challenges you

may be facing and to create a bright and fulfilling future for
yourself.

11: Finding Support During the Healing Process

Finding support during the healing process is an important part of overcoming a toxic relationship and moving forward in a healthy way. It can be challenging to navigate the emotional aftermath of a toxic relationship, and seeking support from trusted friends, family, and professionals can be a helpful way to cope with the challenges you may be facing.

One of the first steps in finding support is to reach out to trusted friends and family members. It can be helpful to talk about your experiences and to share your feelings with people who are supportive and understanding. They can provide emotional support and a listening ear, and they can also be a source of practical help and advice. If you are feeling isolated or alone, reaching out to friends and family can also help to combat these feelings and to connect with others.

Another source of support during the healing process is therapy. Therapy can provide a safe and supportive space to work through your feelings and to develop healthy coping strategies. A therapist can help you to process your experiences, to identify any patterns or issues that may need to be addressed, and to develop healthy communication skills. Therapy can also be a helpful tool for building self-esteem and for learning to trust yourself and your own judgment.

It can also be helpful to seek support from trusted professionals, such as a doctor or a counselor. They can provide practical support and advice, and they can also help to connect you with additional resources and support as needed.

In addition to seeking support from friends, family, and professionals, it can be helpful to find ways to support yourself during the healing process. This may involve finding activities that bring you joy and relaxation, setting aside time for self-care, and finding healthy ways to cope with your feelings. Remember that it's important to be kind to yourself and to give yourself grace as you navigate the challenges of healing.

Finding support during the healing process can be an essential step towards overcoming a toxic relationship and moving forward in a healthy and fulfilling way. Remember that you are not alone, and that there is help and support available to you. Don't be afraid to reach out for help, and remember that you have the strength and resilience to overcome any challenges you may be facing.

It's also important to remember that healing is a process and that it may take time. It's normal to experience a range of emotions as you navigate the aftermath of a toxic relationship, and it's important to be patient with yourself and to give yourself time to heal.

One way to support yourself during the healing process is to seek out healthy and supportive relationships. Surrounding yourself with people who are kind, respectful, and supportive can be an important part of the healing process. These relationships can provide a sense of connection and belonging, and they can also serve as a source of emotional support and encouragement.

Another way to support yourself during the healing process is to engage in activities that bring you joy and relaxation. This may include exercising, spending time in nature, or pursuing a hobby or interest. These activities can help to reduce stress and to improve your overall well-being.

It's also important to remember to take care of your physical health during the healing process. This may involve eating a healthy diet, getting enough sleep, and engaging in regular physical activity. Taking care of your physical health can help to improve your overall well-being and to give you the energy and strength you need to navigate the challenges of healing.

Finally, it's important to remember that you have the strength and resilience to overcome the challenges of a toxic relationship and to create a healthy and fulfilling future for yourself. Don't be afraid to seek help and support as needed, and remember that you deserve to be in a healthy, respectful, and supportive relationship. With time, patience, and self-care, you can heal and move forward in a positive and fulfilling way.

In addition to seeking support from friends, family, and professionals, it can be helpful to find ways to support yourself during the healing process. This may involve finding activities that bring you joy and relaxation, setting aside time for self-care, and finding healthy ways to cope with your feelings. Remember that it's important to be kind to yourself and to give yourself grace as you navigate the challenges of healing.

11: FINDING SUPPORT DURING THE HEALING PRO-CESS

It's also important to remember that healing is a process and that it may take time. It's normal to experience a range of emotions as you navigate the aftermath of a toxic relationship, and it's important to be patient with yourself and to give yourself time to heal.

One way to support yourself during the healing process is to seek out healthy and supportive relationships. Surrounding yourself with people who are kind, respectful, and supportive can be an important part of the healing process. These relationships can provide a sense of connection and belonging, and they can also serve as a source of emotional support and encouragement.

Another way to support yourself during the healing process is to engage in activities that bring you joy and relaxation. This may include exercising, spending time in nature, or pursuing a hobby or interest. These activities can help to reduce stress and to improve your overall well-being.

It's also important to remember to take care of your physical health during the healing process. This may involve eating a healthy diet, getting enough sleep, and engaging in regular physical activity. Taking care of your physical health can help to improve your overall well-being and to give you the energy and strength you need to navigate the challenges of healing.

It's also important to remember that healing is not a linear process, and it's normal to experience setbacks or challenges along the way. It's important to be patient with yourself and to remember that healing takes time. If you find that you are struggling, don't be afraid to seek additional support or to reach out for help. Remember that you are not alone, and that there is help and support available to you.

Finally, it's important to remember that you have the strength and resilience to overcome the challenges of a toxic relationship and to create a healthy and fulfilling future for yourself. Don't be afraid to seek help and support as needed, and remember that you deserve to be in a healthy, respectful, and supportive relationship

12: The Role of Therapy in Dealing with Toxic Relationships

Therapy can be an essential tool for dealing with toxic relationships and for healing from the emotional aftermath of these experiences. A therapist can provide a safe and supportive space to work through your feelings and to develop healthy coping strategies. They can help you to identify any patterns or issues that may need to be addressed, and they can also help you to develop healthy communication skills and to set boundaries.

One of the key benefits of therapy is the opportunity to process your experiences and emotions in a safe and supportive environment. It can be challenging to talk about difficult or painful experiences, and a therapist can provide a nonjudgmental and understanding space to do so. They can help you to explore your thoughts and feelings, and to gain insight into any patterns or behaviors that may be impacting your relationships.

Therapy can also be an important tool for building self-esteem and for learning to trust yourself and your own judgment. A toxic relationship can often leave us feeling uncertain of ourselves or our worth, and a therapist can help you to rebuild your confidence and to develop a positive sense of self.

In addition to these benefits, therapy can also help you to develop healthy coping strategies and to find ways to manage your emotions in a healthy way. This may involve learning new ways of dealing with stress, developing healthy boundaries, or finding healthy ways to cope with difficult emotions.

Finally, therapy can be an important step towards finding closure and moving forward in a healthy and fulfilling way. It can provide a sense of resolution and a sense of understanding, and it can also help you to identify any patterns or issues that may need to be addressed in future relationships.

Overall, therapy can be an essential tool for dealing with toxic relationships and for healing from the emotional aftermath of these experiences. It can provide a safe and supportive space to work through your feelings, to develop healthy coping strategies, and to find closure and a sense of resolution. If you are struggling with a toxic relationship, or if you are dealing with the aftermath of a toxic relationship, consider seeking the support of a therapist or counselor. They can provide you with the tools and support you need to heal and to move forward in a healthy and fulfilling way.

It's important to remember that therapy is a process, and that it may take time to see progress and to find resolution. It's also important to find a therapist that you feel comfortable with and that you feel is a good fit for you. If you are not feeling connected or supported in therapy, it's important to speak up and to consider finding a different therapist.

It's also important to remember that therapy is not a one-size-fits-all approach, and what works for one person may not work for another. It's important to be open to trying different approaches and to finding what works best for you.

Finally, it's important to remember that you are not alone, and that there is help and support available to you. If you are struggling with a toxic relationship, or if you are dealing with the aftermath of a toxic relationship, reach out for help. Remember that you deserve to be in a healthy, respectful, and supportive relationship, and that there is hope for healing and for finding a brighter and more fulfilling future.

It's also important to be aware that therapy is not a quick fix, and that it may take time to see progress and to find resolution. It's important to be patient with yourself and to give yourself time to heal. It's also important to remember that healing is a process, and that it may involve ups and downs and setbacks along the way. It's important to be kind to yourself and to give yourself grace as you navigate the challenges of healing.

In addition to therapy, there are a number of other resources and support systems that can be helpful in dealing with toxic relationships. This may include support groups, self-help books, or online resources. It can be helpful to explore different options and to find what works best for you.

Finally, it's important to remember that healing and recovery are possible, and that you have the strength and resilience to overcome the challenges of a toxic relationship and to create a healthy and fulfilling future for yourself. Don't be afraid to seek help and support, and remember that you deserve to be in a healthy, respectful, and supportive relationship. With time, patience, and self-care, you can heal and move forward in a positive and fulfilling way.

13: The Link Between Childhood Trauma and Toxic Relationships

There is a strong link between childhood trauma and toxic relationships. Childhood trauma refers to any type of negative or harmful experience that occurs during childhood, such as abuse, neglect, or witnessing violence. These experiences can have a significant and lasting impact on a person's emotional and psychological well-being, and they can increase the risk of developing unhealthy relationship patterns in adulthood.

One of the ways that childhood trauma can affect adult relationships is by disrupting the development of healthy attachment styles. Attachment refers to the emotional bond that forms between a child and their caregiver, and it plays a crucial role in the development of a person's sense of self and their ability to form healthy relationships. When a child experiences abuse or neglect, it can disrupt the development of a healthy attachment style and lead to difficulties in forming and maintaining close relationships in adulthood.

Childhood trauma can also impact a person's ability to trust and to regulate their emotions. When a child experiences abuse or neglect, it can shatter their sense of trust and safety in the world. This can lead to difficulties in trusting others and in regulating emotions in adulthood, which can contribute to unhealthy relationship patterns.

Another way that childhood trauma can impact adult relationships is by increasing the risk of developing mental health issues. Childhood trauma is a significant risk factor for the development of mental health issues such as depression, anxiety, and post-traumatic stress disorder (PTSD). These mental health issues can in turn impact a person's ability to form and maintain healthy relationships.

It's important to recognize the link between childhood trauma and toxic relationships, and to understand that healing and recovery are possible. If you have experienced childhood trauma and are struggling in your adult relationships, seeking the support of a therapist or counselor can be an important step towards healing and towards building healthy and fulfilling relationships. Remember that you are not alone, and that there is help and support available to you.

It's also important to recognize that healing from childhood trauma is a process, and that it may take time. It's normal to experience setbacks and challenges along the way, and it's important to be patient with yourself and to give yourself time to heal.

In addition to therapy, there are a number of other resources and support systems that can be helpful in dealing with the aftermath of childhood trauma. This may include support groups, self-help books, or online resources. It can be helpful to explore different options and to find what works best for you.

It's also important to remember that self-care is an essential part of the healing process. Taking care of your physical and emotional well-being is an important step towards healing and towards building healthy and fulfilling relationships. This may involve engaging in activities that bring you joy and relaxation, setting aside time for self-care, and finding healthy ways to cope with your emotions.

Finally, it's important to remember that you are not alone, and that there is help and support available to you. If you are struggling with the aftermath of childhood trauma, reach out for help. Remember that you deserve to be in a healthy, respectful, and supportive relationship, and that there is hope for healing and for finding a brighter and more fulfilling future. With time, patience, and self-care, you can heal and move forward in a positive and fulfilling way.

It's also important to recognize that healing from childhood trauma is not a linear process, and it's normal to experience ups and downs along the way. It's important to be patient with yourself and to give yourself time to heal. It's also important to remember that healing is a journey, and that it's okay to take things one step at a time.

It's also important to recognize that healing from childhood trauma is not something that you have to do alone. There are a number of resources and support systems available to help you on your journey towards healing. This may include therapy, support groups, self-help books, or online resources. It can be helpful to explore different options and to find what works best for you.

It's also important to remember that self-care is an essential part of the healing process. Taking care of your physical and emotional well-being is an important step towards healing and towards building healthy and fulfilling relationships.

13: THE LINK BETWEEN CHILDHOOD TRAUMA AND TOXIC RELATIONSHIPS

This may involve engaging in activities that bring you joy and relaxation, setting aside time for self-care, and finding healthy ways to cope with your emotions.

Finally, it's important to remember that you are not alone, and that there is help and support available to you. If you are struggling with the aftermath of childhood trauma, reach out for help. Remember that you deserve to be in a healthy, respectful, and supportive relationship, and that there is hope for healing and for finding a brighter and more fulfilling future. With time, patience, and self-care, you can heal and move forward in a positive and fulfilling way.

14: The Role of Forgiveness in Healing from a Toxic Relationship

Forgiveness is a process that involves letting go of anger, resentment, and other negative feelings towards someone who has hurt us. It does not mean forgetting or denying the harm that was done, or condoning the behavior of the person who caused the harm. Rather, it is a way of freeing ourselves from the negative emotions that can hold us back and preventing us from moving forward.

Forgiveness can be an important part of the healing process after a toxic relationship. Toxic relationships often involve a high level of betrayal and hurt, and it's natural to feel angry and resentful towards the person who caused us harm. However, holding onto these negative emotions can be damaging to our own well-being and can prevent us from moving forward.

Forgiveness can be a difficult and challenging process, and it's not something that happens overnight. It may involve working through a range of emotions and may require the support of a therapist or counselor. It's important to be patient with yourself and to give yourself time to heal.

14: THE ROLE OF FORGIVENESS IN HEALING FROM A TOXIC RELATIONSHIP

There are a number of different approaches to forgiveness, and it's important to find what works best for you. Some people find it helpful to write about their feelings, while others find it helpful to talk about their experiences with a therapist or trusted friend. It may also be helpful to engage in activities that bring you relaxation and peace, such as meditation or yoga.

Ultimately, forgiveness is a personal choice, and it's important to do what feels right for you. It's okay to take things one step at a time, and it's okay to seek the support of a therapist or counselor if you need it. Remember that forgiveness is a process, and it's normal to have ups and downs along the way. With time, patience, and self-care, you can heal and move forward in a positive and fulfilling way.

It's important to recognize that forgiveness is not a sign of weakness, and it's not about letting someone off the hook for their behavior. Rather, it is a way of freeing ourselves from the negative emotions that can hold us back and preventing us from moving forward. Forgiveness is a way of taking control of our own well-being and of finding peace and healing.

14: THE ROLE OF FORGIVENESS IN HEALING FROM A TOXIC RELATIONSHIP

Forgiveness is also not about condoning or excusing the behavior of the person who caused us harm. It's important to remember that toxic relationships often involve a high level of betrayal and hurt, and it's natural to feel angry and resentful towards the person who caused us harm. However, holding onto these negative emotions can be damaging to our own well-being and can prevent us from moving forward.

It's also important to recognize that forgiveness is a personal choice, and it's not something that everyone is ready for or feels comfortable with. It's okay to take things one step at a time, and it's okay to seek the support of a therapist or counselor if you need it. Remember that healing is a process, and it's normal to have ups and downs along the way.

Finally, it's important to remember that you are not alone, and that there is help and support available to you. If you are struggling with the aftermath of a toxic relationship, reach out for help. Remember that you deserve to be in a healthy, respectful, and supportive relationship, and that there is hope for healing and for finding a brighter and more fulfilling future. With time, patience, and self-care, you can heal and move forward in a positive and fulfilling way.

It's also important to recognize that forgiveness is not a one-time event, and it's not something that happens overnight. It's a process that may take time and may involve working through a range of emotions. It's important to be patient with yourself and to give yourself time to heal.

It's also important to recognize that forgiveness is not a sign of weakness, and it's not about letting someone off the hook for their behavior. Rather, it is a way of freeing ourselves from the negative emotions that can hold us back and preventing us from moving forward. Forgiveness is a way of taking control of our own well-being and of finding peace and healing.

Forgiveness is also not about condoning or excusing the behavior of the person who caused us harm. It's important to remember that toxic relationships often involve a high level of betrayal and hurt, and it's natural to feel angry and resentful towards the person who caused us harm. However, holding onto these negative emotions can be damaging to our own well-being and can prevent us from moving forward.

It's also important to recognize that forgiveness is a personal choice, and it's not something that everyone is ready for or feels comfortable with. It's okay to take things one step at a time, and it's okay to seek the support of a therapist or counselor if you need it. Remember that healing is a process, and it's normal to have ups and downs along the way.

Finally, it's important to remember that you are not alone, and that there is help and support available to you. If you are struggling with the aftermath of a toxic relationship, reach out for help. Remember that you deserve to be in a healthy, respectful, and supportive relationship, and that there is hope for healing and for finding a brighter and more fulfilling future. With time, patience, and self-care, you can heal and move forward in a positive and fulfilling way.

15: Navigating Toxic Relationships in the Workplace

Toxic relationships in the workplace can take many forms, including bullying, harassment, and manipulation. These types of relationships can be harmful to our well-being and can create a negative and unhealthy work environment. It's important to recognize the warning signs of a toxic workplace relationship and to take steps to protect ourselves.

One of the key warning signs of a toxic workplace relationship is a feeling of being mistreated or disrespected. This may involve being ignored, belittled, or excluded from important meetings or decision-making processes. It may also involve being subjected to bullying, harassment, or other forms of abusive behavior.

Another warning sign of a toxic workplace relationship is a feeling of being manipulated or controlled. This may involve being pressured to do things that go against our values or beliefs, or being made to feel guilty for not complying with unreasonable demands. It may also involve being subjected to gaslighting, a type of emotional abuse in which the abuser manipulates the victim into questioning their own perceptions and reality.

371

It's important to recognize these warning signs and to take steps to protect ourselves. This may involve setting boundaries, such as setting limits on the amount of time we are willing to spend with a toxic person or making it clear that we will not tolerate abusive behavior. It may also involve seeking the support of a trusted colleague or supervisor, or seeking the assistance of a human resources representative.

It's also important to remember that we have the right to work in a healthy and respectful environment, and that we deserve to be treated with dignity and respect. If you are struggling with a toxic workplace relationship, it's important to speak up and to seek help. Remember that you are not alone, and that there is support available to you.

Another key strategy for navigating toxic relationships in the workplace is to focus on building a support network. This may involve seeking out the support of colleagues who are understanding and supportive, or joining a professional organization or support group. It may also involve seeking the support of a therapist or counselor who can help you to work through your feelings and to develop healthy coping strategies.

15: NAVIGATING TOXIC RELATIONSHIPS IN THE WORKPLACE

It's also important to remember to take care of your own well-being, both at work and outside of work. This may involve setting aside time for self-care, such as exercising or engaging in activities that bring you joy and relaxation. It may also involve finding healthy ways to cope with stress, such as through meditation or mindfulness practices.

Finally, it's important to remember that we have the power to create positive change in our workplace, and that we can be agents of positive transformation. This may involve speaking up about toxic behavior or working to create a more positive and supportive work culture. It may also involve finding ways to advocate for ourselves and for others who may be struggling with toxic workplace relationships.

Remember that you are not alone, and that there is help and support available to you. If you are struggling with a toxic workplace relationship, don't be afraid to seek help and to speak up. Remember that you deserve to work in a healthy and respectful environment, and that you have the power to create positive change in your workplace. With time, patience, and self-care, you can navigate the challenges of toxic relationships and create a brighter and more fulfilling future.

It's also important to remember that it's not always possible to change or to fix a toxic workplace relationship. In some cases, the best course of action may be to remove ourselves from the toxic environment. This may involve finding a new job, transferring to a different department, or seeking the assistance of a human resources representative.

Leaving a toxic workplace relationship can be a difficult and challenging decision, and it's important to carefully weigh the pros and cons. It may be helpful to seek the advice of a trusted friend, family member, or therapist, or to discuss your options with a human resources representative.

It's also important to remember that leaving a toxic workplace relationship does not mean that we have failed or that we are weak. Rather, it is a way of taking control of our own well-being and of finding a healthy and supportive work environment. It's a way of putting ourselves and our well-being first, and it's a brave and important step towards finding fulfillment and happiness.

If you are considering leaving a toxic workplace relationship, it's important to remember that you are not alone, and that there is help and support available to you. Remember that you deserve to work in a healthy and respectful environment, and that there is hope for finding a brighter and more fulfilling future. With time, patience, and self-care, you can navigate the challenges of toxic relationships and create a brighter and more fulfilling future.

16: The Role of Self-Care in Dealing with Toxic Relationships

Self-care is an essential part of the process of dealing with toxic relationships. Toxic relationships can take a toll on our well-being and can leave us feeling drained, anxious, and overwhelmed. It's important to remember that taking care of ourselves is not selfish, and that it is an important part of the healing process.

There are many different ways to practice self-care, and it's important to find what works best for you. Some ideas for self-care may include:

− Engaging in activities that bring you joy and relaxation, such as hobbies, exercise, or creative pursuits

− Setting aside time for rest and relaxation, such as taking a warm bath or reading a book

− Eating a healthy and balanced diet, and getting enough sleep

− Setting boundaries, such as setting limits on the amount of time we spend with a toxic person or setting limits on our own workload

16: THE ROLE OF SELF-CARE IN DEALING WITH TOXIC RELATIONSHIPS

– Seeking the support of friends, family, or a therapist

It's important to remember that self-care is not a one-time event, but rather a continuous process. It's important to make self-care a priority, and to set aside time for self-care on a regular basis.

Self-care is also about taking care of our emotional and mental well-being, as well as our physical well-being. It may involve finding healthy ways to cope with difficult emotions, such as through journaling, talking to a therapist, or engaging in mindfulness practices.

Ultimately, self-care is about taking care of ourselves and about finding ways to nourish and support our well-being. It's about recognizing that we deserve to be healthy and happy, and about taking the steps needed to create a fulfilling and positive life.

It's important to remember that self-care is not about denying or ignoring our problems, but rather about finding healthy ways to cope with them. It's about finding balance and about taking care of ourselves so that we can better navigate the challenges that life brings.

Self-care is also about setting boundaries and about learning to say no when necessary. This may involve setting limits on the amount of time we spend with a toxic person or setting limits on our own workload. It may also involve setting boundaries with ourselves, such as by not allowing ourselves to become overwhelmed or by setting aside time for rest and relaxation.

It's important to recognize that self-care is a personal process, and what works for one person may not work for another. It's important to experiment and to find what works best for you. It may be helpful to keep a self-care journal, in which you can track your self-care activities and reflect on what works and what doesn't.

It's also important to remember that self-care is not a sign of weakness, and it's not something to feel guilty about. It's about taking care of ourselves and about finding ways to nourish and support our well-being. It's about recognizing that we deserve to be healthy and happy, and about taking the steps needed to create a fulfilling and positive life.

Remember to be kind to yourself and to give yourself permission to take care of yourself. Remember that you are not alone, and that there is help and support available to you. With time, patience, and self-care, you can navigate the challenges of toxic relationships and create a brighter and more fulfilling future.

One of the most important aspects of self-care is learning to recognize and to set boundaries. Boundaries are about learning to say no when necessary, and about protecting our own well-being and emotional needs. It's important to recognize that it's okay to prioritize our own needs, and that it's okay to put ourselves first.

Setting boundaries can be especially important in toxic relationships, as toxic individuals often push against boundaries and attempt to manipulate or control their victims. It's important to recognize that we have the right to set limits on how we are treated, and that we have the right to protect ourselves from abuse and mistreatment.

It's important to remember that setting boundaries is not about being aggressive or confrontational, but rather about communicating our own needs and limits in a clear and respectful way. It may be helpful to practice saying no in a non-confrontational way, such as by saying something like,

"I'm sorry, but I'm not comfortable with that" or "I'm sorry, but I can't do that right now."

It's also important to remember that setting boundaries is a process, and that it may take time to learn what works best for us. It may be helpful to seek the support of a therapist or counselor, who can help us to develop healthy boundary-setting skills and to cope with any challenges that may arise.

Remember that you deserve to be treated with respect and dignity, and that it's okay to prioritize your own well-being. With time, patience, and self-care, you can learn to set healthy boundaries and to create a brighter and more fulfilling future.

17: The Importance of Setting Healthy Relationship Expectations

One of the key factors in creating healthy and fulfilling relationships is setting healthy expectations. Healthy relationship expectations are about knowing what we want and need in a relationship, and about communicating these needs clearly and respectfully to our partners.

Having healthy relationship expectations can help us to create more fulfilling and satisfying relationships, and can also help us to avoid toxic or unhealthy relationships. It's important to recognize that we have the right to expect respect, honesty, and kindness from our partners, and that we have the right to set limits on how we are treated.

It's also important to recognize that our relationship expectations may change over time, and that it's okay to reassess our needs and wants as our lives and circumstances change. It's important to communicate these changes to our partners, and to be open and honest about what we need and want in a relationship.

One of the key challenges in setting healthy relationship expectations is learning to communicate effectively with our partners. This may involve practicing active listening, asking open-ended questions, and using "I" statements to express our own feelings and needs. It's also important to be open to compromise and to be willing to find solutions that work for both partners.

It's important to remember that setting healthy relationship expectations is a continuous process, and that it requires ongoing communication and effort. It's about finding what works best for both partners, and about creating a relationship that is fulfilling and supportive for both people. With time, patience, and communication, we can create healthy and fulfilling relationships that bring joy and happiness into our lives.

Another important aspect of setting healthy relationship expectations is being aware of our own needs and wants. It's important to take the time to think about what we need and want in a relationship, and to be honest with ourselves about our own needs and boundaries. This may involve reflecting on past relationships and on what worked and what didn't work for us, and it may involve seeking the support of a therapist or counselor.

It's also important to recognize that our needs and wants may change over time, and that it's okay to reassess and to communicate these changes to our partners. It's important to remember that it's okay to have needs and boundaries, and that it's important to advocate for ourselves and to communicate our needs and wants clearly and respectfully.

It's also important to recognize that setting healthy relationship expectations is not about trying to control or manipulate our partners, but rather about creating a relationship that is healthy and fulfilling for both people. It's about finding a balance and about being open and honest about our own needs and wants.

Remember that setting healthy relationship expectations is an ongoing process, and that it requires ongoing communication and effort. With time, patience, and communication, we can create healthy and fulfilling relationships that bring joy and happiness into our lives.

It's also important to recognize that setting healthy relationship expectations does not guarantee a problem-free relationship. All relationships have challenges and conflicts, and it's important to be prepared to work through these challenges and to communicate openly and honestly with our partners.

One of the key strategies for dealing with conflicts and challenges in a relationship is to practice good communication skills. This may involve practicing active listening, asking open-ended questions, and using "I" statements to express our own feelings and needs. It's also important to be open to compromise and to be willing to find solutions that work for both partners.

It's important to remember that conflicts and challenges are a normal part of any relationship, and that it's okay to disagree. It's important to recognize that it's okay to have different viewpoints, and that it's important to respect and value each other's perspectives.

It's also important to recognize that it's okay to seek outside help if needed, such as through therapy or counseling. Seeking outside help can be especially beneficial if we are struggling to communicate effectively or if we are having difficulty resolving conflicts.

17: THE IMPORTANCE OF SETTING HEALTHY RELA-
TIONSHIP EXPECTATIONS

Ultimately, setting healthy relationship expectations is about creating a relationship that is healthy and fulfilling for both people. It's about finding a balance and about being open and honest about our own needs and wants. With time, patience, and communication, we can navigate the challenges of any relationship and create a brighter and more fulfilling future.

18: Creating a Support System for Long-Term Recovery from Toxic Relationships

One of the key factors in long-term recovery from toxic relationships is building a strong and supportive network of people. Having a supportive network of friends, family, and other loved ones can provide a sense of connection, belonging, and emotional support, and can be an important source of strength and resilience.

There are many different ways to build a supportive network, and it's important to find what works best for you. Some ideas for building a supportive network may include:

– Reaching out to friends and family members who are supportive and understanding

– Joining a support group or a community organization

– Seeking the support of a therapist or counselor

– Participating in activities that bring you joy and connection, such as hobbies or volunteer work

– Seeking out the support of a trusted mentor or role model

18: CREATING A SUPPORT SYSTEM FOR LONG-TERM RECOVERY FROM TOXIC RELATIONSHIPS

It's important to remember that building a supportive network is an ongoing process, and that it requires effort and time. It's important to make a conscious effort to connect with others and to nurture our relationships.

It's also important to remember that it's okay to reach out for help when we need it. It's important to recognize that we don't have to face our challenges alone, and that there is help and support available to us.

Remember that building a supportive network is an important part of the healing process, and that it's okay to ask for help when we need it. With time, patience, and effort, we can build a strong and supportive network of people who can provide the support and connection that we need to heal and to move forward.

It's also important to recognize that building a supportive network may involve seeking the support of professionals, such as therapists or counselors. Professional support can be especially helpful if we are struggling to cope with the aftermath of a toxic relationship, or if we are having difficulty processing and healing from the experience.

18: CREATING A SUPPORT SYSTEM FOR LONG-TERM RECOVERY FROM TOXIC RELATIONSHIPS

Therapy and counseling can provide a safe and supportive space to explore our thoughts, feelings, and experiences, and can help us to develop healthy coping skills and to gain a greater understanding of ourselves and our relationships. It can also be a helpful resource for learning healthy communication skills and for setting healthy boundaries.

It's important to remember that therapy and counseling are not a sign of weakness, and that they are an important resource for anyone who is struggling. It's important to be open to seeking help, and to recognize that therapy and counseling can be an important part of the healing process.

Remember that building a supportive network is an ongoing process, and that it requires effort and time. It's important to make a conscious effort to connect with others and to nurture our relationships. With time, patience, and effort, we can build a strong and supportive network of people who can provide the support and connection that we need to heal and to move forward.

It's also important to recognize that building a supportive network may involve finding support within ourselves. This may involve learning healthy coping skills, such as mindfulness practices or healthy ways to express and process our emotions. It may also involve finding activities that bring us joy and relaxation, such as hobbies or creative pursuits.

Self-care is an important part of building a supportive network within ourselves, and it's about taking care of our own well-being and emotional needs. It's about finding ways to nourish and support our own well-being, and about recognizing that we deserve to be healthy and happy.

It's important to remember that building a supportive network is an ongoing process, and that it requires effort and time. It's important to make a conscious effort to connect with others and to nurture our relationships. It's also important to make time for self-care and to prioritize our own well-being. With time, patience, and effort, we can build a strong and supportive network of people and find the strength and resilience to heal and to move forward.

Thank You

As we reach the end of this book, I want to say thanks for reading this book.

I want to get this information out to as many people as possible. If you found this book helpful, I would greatly appreciate you leaving me a review. This helps others find the book as well.

Disclaimer

This document is geared towards providing exact and reliable information in regards to the topic and issue covered. The publication is sold on the idea that the publisher is not required to render an accounting, officially permitted, or otherwise, qualified services. If advice is necessary, legal, financial, medical or professional, a practiced individual in the profession should be ordered.

This information is not presented by a financial or medical practitioner and is for entertainment, educational and informational purposes only. The content is not intended as a substitute for professional medical advice, diagnosis, or treatment. Always seek the advice of your physician or other qualified health care provider with any questions you may have regarding a medical condition. Never disregard professional medical advice or delay in seeking it because of something you have read.

The information provided herein is stated to be truthful and consistent, in that any liability, in terms of inattention or otherwise, by any usage or abuse of any policies, processes, or directions contained within is the solitary and utter responsibility of the recipient reader. Under no circumstances

DISCLAIMER

will any legal responsibility or blame be held against the
publisher for any reparation, damages, or monetary loss
due to the information herein, either directly or indirectly.

www.ingramcontent.com/pod-product-compliance
Lightning Source LLC
Chambersburg PA
CBHW062113020426
42335CB00013B/942